ESSAYS BY DIVERS HANDS

BEING THE

TRANSACTIONS

OF THE

ROYAL SOCIETY OF LITERATURE
OF THE UNITED KINGDOM

NEW SERIES

VOL. XVII

EDITED BY E. H. W. MEYERSTEIN, M.A., F.R.S.L.

ESSAY INDEX IN REPRINT

Core Collection Books, inc.
GREAT NECK NEW YORK

FIRST PUBLISHED 1938
REPRINTED 1978

INTERNATIONAL STANDARD BOOK NUMBER 0-8486-3029-7

PRINTED IN THE UNITED STATES OF AMERICA

CONTENTS

INTRODUCTION.

By E. H. W. MEYERSTEIN, M.A., F.R.S.L.

THE essays, or lectures, that constitute this seventeenth volume are linked by no common purpose, and it would indeed be uncritical to deduce one from them. Doubtless all partake of the anxiety of our time, and the yearning of those born in more stable periods, as well as younger spirits, for a watch-tower immune from perils above or below. Precise ascertained extrovert truth (in a word, scholarship), now that the unconscious is the game of so many, would seem to offer the safest foothold in a world that is crumbling about our ears with no guarantee of coming to a real end. But the prudent user of this book, as of its predecessors, taking its scholarship for granted, the labour of accredited hands, will, reading for pleasure, be on the watch for the *aperçu*, the flash of illuminating sense, rarely the mere scholar's prerogative. It is the introducer's business to anticipate that, to some extent, and a faithful editor will not spoil a reader's pleasure by seeing too much.

The brilliant *declamatio* of Professor Gordon, so pregnant with sly university wit, asks no commentary. Yet, arising from his light-hearted consideration of what for some, at least, is a tragic theme, the lives of authors, two pertinent thoughts press on any sensitive

mind ; the critic of the future will have to weigh
them carefully :

    1. The effect on the quality and production of
literature by the acceptance of the modern social
and economic principle that the payment of
authors constitutes the reality of their perfor-
mances.

    2. The effect on the same of the vast and
increasing quantity of women writers, and the
consequent inevitable presentation of truth in
poetry and prose from a feminine angle. As far
back as 1887, in a paper read to the Shelley
Society, John Todhunter observed that the next
century would be the century of women.

Perhaps these interconnected ideas belong rather
to the history of publishing or publicity ; they appear
to me latent in the Vice-Chancellor of Oxford's
remarks on a Victorian authoress's attitude to
payment.

In the Tredegar Memorial Lecture Mr. F. L. Lucas
finds a panacea for the unrest of the stay-at-home, no
less than the globe-trotter, in the narratives of
travellers in Greece from Pausanias to Lord Byron.
His gracious, unhurried, regretful periods, colourful
with citation, achieve his purpose admirably. They
take one reader, at least, back to a book that first
revealed for him the persistence of pagan tradition in
the modern world, that very personal study in
survivals, ' Modern Greek Folklore and Ancient Greek
Religion ', by another distinguished son of Cambridge,
the late J. C. Lawson. Mr. Lucas, as a literary
traveller, has reaffirmed the beauty of ' Death's
Jest-Book ' and brought the poetry of Beddoes

nearer to the mind of to-day, and here too he awakens
the dead, as he succinctly says, " to make our lives
fully living ".   " Travel teaches toleration," wrote
Disraeli in ' Contarini Fleming '.

Professor Hotson, we know, wears his weight of
learning like a flower, and to attempt to epitomize
his paper on a minor Elizabethan poet (with how
much discovered by the way !) would be to make of
it a weed.   Of him, in this connection, can be said
what Propertius may have said of Acanthis :

> " Exornabat opus verbis ceu blanda perurit
> Saxosamque forat sedula *caltha* viam."

The marigold of the Romans may not have been a
marsh plant ;   after reading this memorial to T.
Cutwode, alternatively Tailboys Dymoke, the friend
of Daniel, the possible " original " of Mercutio, the
editor is inspired to hazard a conjecture that not
culpa, lympha, gutta, cura, no, not even the German
mole (*talpa*) is the correct reading in that *locus
vexatissimus.*   So contagious the perfume of this
marigold !   The way of scholarship seems stony no
longer when explored with such a guide.   ' The
Transformed Metamorphosis ' is in the same metre as
' Caltha Poetarum or the Bumble Bee ' ;   let us
hope for Professor Hotson's elucidation of *that.*   How
far have Tudor studies advanced since 1815, when
Richard Heber was content to offer ' T. Cutwode '
to the Roxburghe Club with no commentary at all !

Sir William Craigie's eloquent excursus on dialect
in literature might be appraised from many points of
view.   That which most readily suggests itself is that,
in an age where facility of transport links distant

places so speedily that their dialects, like their
produce, tend to be assimilated to a common standard,
we have yet such an interest in language among us
that a dictionary of *argot*, nearly half as long as one
volume of ' The Shorter Oxford English Dictionary ',
has passed into a second edition, with additions,
almost at once. It is definitely (to use current
jargon) when language loses its earthiness and
raciness that the scientific exploration of it begins.
The age of Plautus was long past when the ' Noctes
Atticae ' were written, and both our prose and our
verse had entered on their most standardised and
stiffest period when Johnson started his heroic task.

Mr. Gawsworth, in his scrutiny of the myth that
has enveloped the pathetic figure of Ernest Dowson,
performs a meritorious act of literary mine-sweeping.
A bohemian legend is the entertainment-tax demanded
almost inevitably of the celibate poet of love, and,
except the poet be something of a poseur and deliberately create his own, the dissipation of the mists
of dissipation is attended by difficulties happily
surmounted by the lecturer. Verlaine's *Vous n'avez
rien compris à ma simplicité* might more truly have
been said by the self-effacing author of ' The Pierrot
of the Minute ' ; but if a man's verses tell of " the
roses and the wine ", human nature, nine-tenths
materialistic, will seldom rest satisfied with " the
wild expenses of a poet's brain ", but must needs
invent what it cannot prove.

The last piece, the contribution of a distinguished
visitor, Mr. Sándor de Hegedüs, stands on a slightly
different footing. It is an *éloge* of the Magyar national
lyrist Petőfi, who, though still little read in this

country, found an English translator in Sir John Bowring as early as seventeen years after his heroic death. Through it speaks a patriotism undeterred and undetermined by territorial boundaries. If, to use Kantian language, a regulative principle be required for the present agitated state of the world, it may perhaps be found here. A sensitive reader will follow the very sincerely expressed paragraphs with his heart rather than his head, though the writer is as accredited as his fellow hands. It is not the first time that Petőfi's name has appeared in these ' Transactions '. I have found a reference to a paper on him by Mrs. Arthur Ginever (*née* Ilona de Győry), but absence of year and index must leave its excavation to the Hungarian student.

Accredited hands ! The presentation of what follows has been a curious pleasure. The editor is left wondering, so swift, so capricious is the rise and fall of contemporary reputations, which among these lecturers will be suffered to pass as persons of weight and learning a generation hence, or whether their introducer will be accorded more literary credit than his instant task, if indeed that. The words of Goethe, translated by Shelley, leap to the mind :

" but I must vanish.
I am a Dilettante curtain-lifter."

THE LIVES OF AUTHORS.

By G. S. Gordon, M.A., LL.D., D.Litt., F.R.S.L.

I have often asked myself what it is that makes people so curious about authors. Many readers, of course, are not ; they take their dose of print as they take their tobacco or their meals, and regard the name of the author as only one of many trademarks. They order in almost precisely the same spirit another box of cigarettes and another P. G. Wodehouse. To this enormous class of readers the life of a professional author, when they think of it at all (which is seldom), seems as odd and remote as the life of a financier or a company promoter does to me. I accept the fact and the mystery of money as they accept the fact and the mystery of books, and we both leave it at that.

I have, let me say, no· quarrel with this class of readers. Indeed, I like them. They are the clay we grow our roses in. They are the imperturbable force of gravity which keeps our mimic world, the coterie world of the Arts, from flying off into fragments. They keep authors in their place at the same time as they contribute to their support. Being purely customers, they steadily remind us of what authors and their votaries have often tended, I think unhealthily, to conceal : the plain fact that, whatever else it is, professional authorship at any rate is in

one important aspect of it a business, in which something, however valuable, is offered for sale. The
price may be ludicrous—a few coins for an immortal
composition ; but still we are asked to buy. We put
down our money for it ; it does not come to us in a
vision, or with the dew. Even a poet sells his works,
if he can, and has been known to compare his takings
with those of other poets. Lord Tennyson had made
great sacrifices for his art ; he was a *vates sacer*, a
dedicated bard. But he knew exactly what Long-
fellow's publishers gave him as a retaining fee, and it
annoyed him extremely, and justifiably, that his
own was less.

There remains, of our gigantic reading public, a
still considerable portion which looks behind the
commodity, and cannot help being interested in the
authors of the books it reads. It is a natural
curiosity, though some decry it as impertinent. " You
have the book," they say; "why muddle the impression by calling in the author ? " But most books that
are worth anything are a barter of experience, and
it is not unreasonable, I think, that one should wish
to test sincerity, to check credentials. I believe that
women, on the whole, have been quicker to ask for
this than men, which is what we should expect.
They have very good and particular reasons for being
interested in sincerity. Women less often than men
forget the speaker in the speech, and they have always
been more attracted by persons than by principles.
In the matter of authors, and more especially of the
lives of authors, this bias of women has been important.
" I have observed," says Addison, in that well-known
first sentence of the *Spectator*, " that a reader seldom

peruses a book with pleasure until he knows whether the writer of it be a black or a fair man, of a mild or choleric disposition, married or a bachelor, with other particulars of the like nature that conduce very much to the right understanding of an author." This, no doubt, was mainly Addison's fun, but it was also a recognition of something genuine and novel. The empire of the leisured reading public had begun its slow passage into the hands of women, where, in England and America at any rate, it now rests. As women became readers, let us say, the lives of authors became interesting. For it is not, I would have you observe, a male curiosity that Addison describes. The particulars cited are not men's particulars. " Black " or " fair ", " married " or " a bachelor ", no male reader cares twopence about this. The curiosity is feminine. I believe that the persistent pressure of this natural inquisitiveness has had almost as much to do with the development of literary biography as the scholarly and historical interests of men.

What Addison could not foresee was that this child of curiosity should so marvellously outgrow its parents, that the lives of authors should become, as in the last hundred years they have become, an exciting topic in themselves, quite apart from the works which presumably they illustrate. Boswell's ' Life of Johnson ' is read from many motives, and any motive will do, but rarely, even now, because it conduces to an understanding of ' The Rambler '. The lives of Burns and Cowper, of Byron and Shelley, of Keats and Wordsworth, are not only by many people better known than their works ; they are

actually better known than the lives of even the
greatest of their contemporaries who did not also
happen to be famous authors. And I ask myself
why.

Whatever the reason, the thing itself is revolutionary. Until the eighteenth century or the closing
years of the seventeenth, an author, certainly an
English author, to have his life written, had to be
notable, as a rule, in some other way. He must be a
statesman, or a soldier, or a divine, and under cover of
this distinction his literary life might be portrayed. I
wish that this plain historical fact were better known.
We should have been saved so much nonsense about
the " mystery " of the life of Shakespeare, the great
Stratford riddle.   Beyond the miracle of transcendent
genius there is no " mystery " about Shakespeare's
life. Biographically his state is normal. We know
less about his elder contemporary Spenser, who moved
in official circles, and for many years had been by
general consent the greatest poet of his age. Literary
biography, as we understand it, was not yet a felt
need.   Even a century later it seemed to be no one's
business to write a life of John Dryden, the ruling
writer of his day, and we know in consequence very
little about him beyond what he has told us himself.
What Johnson says of Dryden may be said, indeed, of
nearly all our English writers before the eighteenth
century :   " His   contemporaries,   however   they
reverenced his genius, left his life unwritten ; and
nothing therefore can be known beyond what casual
mention and uncertain tradition have supplied."

We have reversed all that, and reversed it so
violently that it is now not the authors who are in

shadow, but those very public men who formerly obscured them. For one person to-day who knows anything, for example, of the lives of the great statesmen and other public characters of the last two centuries, of the Walpoles and Chathams, the Castlereaghs and Palmerstons, there are fifty who know the lives, or something about the lives, of the distinguished contemporary writers whom these potentates ignored or patronized. And the reason? Are authors, as being by nature less reticent than other men, accomplices in the matter? To some extent, no doubt, they are, and to an increasing degree. Are they also, possibly, more interesting in themselves? I am inclined to suppose they must be, though, if this be so, it is a fairly modern discovery. The test of one's contemporaries gives rather doubtful results. Your experience may be different. But the professional authors of my acquaintance, the eminent living writers whom I am privileged to know, have never seemed to me, as a class, the most interesting men extant. Yet, when they die, the same thing, no doubt, will happen. Their often greater contemporaries in other walks of life will sink to a meagre entry in the biographical dictionaries, if indeed they are mentioned there at all, while researchers rake the dustbins for every rejected scrap from the writer's pen, and pursue him in biography from the premonitions of the nursery to the last lessons of the grave.

The holding acquired by authors in the biographical stock of the country is thus immense, for the effects of the new interest have been retrospective. The ' Dictionary of National Biography ' affords a rough and ready test of biographical standing. Apply it, and you will find that, in this particular competition, no class can hold a candle to the authors. As Walter Raleigh used to say, the gates that refuse to open for a minor canon open easily for the minor poet. Even the sailor, the soldier, the diplomatist must do magnificently more than his duty, or disastrously less, to gain admittance there. The rich merchant, who controlled in his time the prosperity of thousands, is turned away, while the poor author stretches himself at ease on the lap of posterity. Grub Street gives up its dead. We had a King in England once who, unless he is traduced, died of eating too many lampreys. We had also a poor author who died of eating too many red herrings. In the biographical dictionaries poor Greene's red herrings now compete for immortality with the lampreys of King Henry.

I am not, of course, complaining. I do not fight with the tides. I only remark that biographical immortality seems to be purchased at different rates, and that the average rate for authors is not high. Their minimum rate is perhaps the lowest there is.

Can I explain it ? Not entirely. To some extent, no doubt, there is trade unionism in the matter : authors write up authors. But in the end, I suppose, it is *expression* that does it. The smallest author who sincerely expresses his pin-point of a soul has, on this reckoning, more chance of survival than the dominant man who has never learned to confess, to commit himself to paper. So many great men are silent, or ill-equipped with words. Some of the most interesting lives of the last hundred years have been the lives of business men, but who is to write them ? They cannot or will not do it themselves, and no author can do it for them. They survive as a rule only in the name and tradition of their firms, or in the titles of their benefactions. Hazlitt, it appears, was right. Authors are a longer-lived race than other men, because " words are the only things that last for ever ".

Yet the authors, to do them justice, have never been happy about it. They know that action, ' fine doing ', is the finest thing in the world. " We talked of war. *Johnson :* Every man thinks meanly of himself for not having been a soldier, or not having been at sea. *Boswell :* Lord Mansfield does not. *Johnson :* Sir, if Lord Mansfield were in a company of General Officers and Admirals who have been in service, he would shrink ; he'd wish to creep under the table. *Boswell :* No ; he'd think he could *try* them all. *Johnson :* . . . No, Sir ; were Socrates and Charles the Twelfth of Sweden both present in any company, and Socrates to say, ' Follow me, and hear a lecture on philosophy ' ; and Charles, laying his hand on his sword, to say, ' Follow me, and dethrone the Czar ' ; a man would be ashamed to follow Socrates. Sir, the impression is universal ; yet it is strange." Just so, in Disraeli's ' Lothair ', " the standing committee of the Holy Alliance of Peoples all rose, although they were extreme Republicans, when the General entered. Such " (says the author) " is the magical influence of a man of action over men of the pen and the tongue ".

The votaries of literature tend to conceal these things and to assign a contemporary altitude to authors which now and then, indeed, may ideally have been theirs, but which in real life few of any generation have either possessed or claimed. There is a widespread

habit among literary historians of naming what
we call an 'Age' after its principal author—the
Age of Johnson, the Age of Tennyson, and so on.
It is a harmless enough habit when confined to its
immediate purpose, and it is very convenient. But
it is based, of course, on a historical unreality, and
when thoughtlessly used, as it very often is, encourages
the oddest misconceptions.

One reason, and not the least, for the slow development of literary biography was the doubtful standing
of the professional author. To write for money was
not genteel. Even so late as the middle of last
century, Charlotte Yonge, for example, that popular
Victorian authoress, could not touch her profits.
A Yonge couldn't do that. Then the life, the mode
of existence, of a professional author has few of those
regular and tangible signs by which a community
recognizes the props and pillars of its society. The
very advantages of an author's trade work against him
here. Let me recite them to you in the words of
Trollope :

" There is perhaps no career of life," he says, " so
charming as that of a successful man of letters. In
the first place, you have such freedom : If you like
the town, live in the town, and do your work there ;
if you like the country, choose the country. It may
be done on the top of a mountain or in the bottom
of a pit. It is compatible with the rolling of the sea
and the motion of a railway. The clergyman, the
lawyer, the doctor, the member of Parliament, the
clerk in a public office, the tradesman, and even his
assistant in the shop, must dress in accordance with
certain fixed laws [the year was 1876]; but the author

need sacrifice to no grace, hardly even to Propriety. He is subject to no bonds such as those which bind other men. Who else is free from all shackles as to hours ? The judge must sit at ten, and the attorney-general, who is making his £20,000 a year, must be there with his bag. The Prime Minister must be in his place on that weary front bench shortly after prayers, and must sit there, either asleep or awake, even though —— or —— should be addressing the House. During all that Sunday which he maintains should be a day of rest, the active clergyman is toiling like a galley-slave. The actor, when eight o'clock comes, is bound to his footlights. The Civil Service clerk must sit there from ten till four—unless his office be fashionable, when twelve to six is just as heavy on him. The author may do his work at five in the morning when he is fresh from his bed, or at three in the morning before he goes there. . . ."

So Trollope runs on, and it is nearly all true. But of course, this very freedom, by removing the author from public check and control, only intensified the common doubt. Even to this day, among simple or old-fashioned people, the profession of author is apt to seem a dubious trade. When Thomas Hardy died, one of his cousins (I think it was), Miss Teresa Hardy, said to a reporter : " Poor Tom ! he was a clever boy, but I never thought he would have taken to writing. Writing, I think, is not a respectable way of earning a living." Hardy, you see, had been bred an architect, and his family, it appears, would have preferred that he had remained one. So in Kirriemuir, some fifty years ago, there was consternation among the village elders when James

Barrie set up as writer and as nothing else. " Mercy be here ! " said the old ladies, " An author ! And him an M.A. ! " He might so preferably, with that appendage, have been a schoolmaster, a doctor, a clergyman—good visible occupations. In turning professional author he was thought to have stepped down.

This very natural feeling is no doubt fast disappearing. But it still lingers in unexpected quarters. When Mr. J. B. Priestley was writing ' The Good Companions ' in the village of Church Hanborough, and spending long days thumping out that joyous work on his typewriter, the villagers, in the absence of any other explanation, felt obliged to conclude the worst, and were divided in opinion whether he was a bookmaker or a begging letter-writer.

To return to the public interest in authors. One of the principal reasons for the change of fashion in that matter is the prevalent notion that the writer of an interesting book must be interesting in himself. Authors, of course, know better ; it is so painfully possible that his book is the only interesting thing about him. Dr. Johnson was once asked by a certain Mrs. Cotterell to introduce her to a celebrated writer, and it is recorded that he dissuaded her from the attempt. " Dearest madam," he said, " you had better let it alone ; the best part of every author is in general to be found in his book." So convinced was he of this that he recommends, indeed, to authors the great advantage of keeping out of sight: "It has been long the custom of the oriental monarchs to hide themselves. . . . and to be known to their subjects only by their edicts. The same policy is no less necessary

to him that writes." " A transition," he concludes,
" from an author's book to his conversation is too
often like an entrance into a large city, after a distant
prospect. Remotely, we see nothing but spires of
temples, and turrets of palaces, and imagine it the
residence of splendour, grandeur, and magnificence ;
but, when we have passed the gates, we find it
perplexed with narrow passages, disgraced with
despicable cottages, embarrassed with obstructions,
and clouded with smoke."

Since Johnson's time the exploration of those
narrow passages in the lives of authors has become
one of our literary industries. The results, on the
whole, though highly interesting, have not tended to
edification, and to a rather serious extent have been
actually, I think, misleading : fuller of quarrels and
debts and love affairs, things common to us all, than
of the specific and distinguishing business of authorship. Most modern lives of the poets resemble,
indeed, the daily press in their addiction to sensa-
sional episodes and their neglect of what is normal.
We read in our morning newspaper of seductions,
abandonments, and divorces, but of the normal work
of Cupid, of the vast average married happiness of
the nation, not a word. So it is very often with these
lives of authors. Maurois' ' Ariel,' for example, which
set or helped to set a fashion, tells us quite charmingly
all manner of things about Shelley ; but the most
important thing of all, how and why he was a poet,
and how and when he did his work, is hardly touched.

It is the peculiar gift of responsible literary
biography that it enables us to see our man twice,
once in his writings and again in his life. Do they fit,

we ask ?   And if not, why don't they ?   The prime
example in recent years has been the biography of
Wordsworth.   A little scandal long suppressed, but at
last revealed, has seemed to renovate by its suggestion
the whole study of this poet.   The pleasure of finding
that Wordsworth had a past, that his youth resembled
so much less than had been supposed the middle age
of other men !   The thing itself, the *liaison*, is of quite
secondary importance, but it is a link in the tangled
chain of interpretation.   Every student of Wordsworth has had to look at him afresh, and has found
that he was looking at him in a new way.   The poet's
indignation may be conceived could he have known
of these disclosures, and of the knot of researchers
who have written books about them.   In such matters
he was jealous, and as late as 1820 still regarded
Boswell's ' Life of Johnson ' as an ungentlemanly
book, an unwarrantable interference with the inti-
macies of private life.   Tennyson later, and Browning,
so far at least as their own privacy was concerned,
took much the same view.   But I am afraid it is
useless ; the more eminent the writer the less privacy
must he expect.   The relation between a poet and
a reader, says Mr. Garrod, is not, and was never
meant to be, the relation, as we call it, between one
gentleman and another.   It would be at least as true to
say that " a poet is a man who throws a stone at your
window (if he is a poet of any power he breaks it).
You run to the window, or you pursue him down the
street, because you, quite properly, want to know
something more about him than the stone.   A great
poet is not an ordinary occurrence . . .   A great
poet is a challenge ; and he must abide our question.

He may, no doubt, claim certain reserves, just as he claims copyright—and perhaps for about the same period. . . . " But, in general, " we are entitled to all the talk, small and great, about great poets which we can scrape together ; with this proviso, that we make a proper use of it : that we can, and do, relate it to the primary fact about them, namely that they *are* great."

I think this is true, and that a poet is less than most men in a position to object. For poets them- selves have never been good at " suppressing " ; indeed it is one of their plainest duties not to suppress. A corresponding candour may fairly be looked for from their biographers. The biographer of a great poet, so long as he knows what he is about, should be as bad at suppressing as the poet himself.

I suppose that biography, whether of authors or of other men, was never better understood, at any rate, than it is to-day. To a more rigorous research, and a much higher degree of candour than was usual even twenty years ago, it has added, not always culpably, the engaging methods of the novel. There will still, no doubt, be family biographies, glossy, high-minded, and unsatisfactory. There will still be examples, though fewer and more furtive, of those biographies which spoke of " drawing a veil ", and how the poets have suffered from them is too painful a story for this occasion. I can remember our derision as undergraduates over the concluding sentence of a short biography of Marlowe in what was then a standard work, ' The History of English Dramatic Literature' by William Adolphus Ward. The sentence was this : " No comment is needed on such a life with such an end." It is some measure of our progress not only in literature but in life that to-day no comment would be needed on such a biographer.

In the biographical renaissance of our times a prominent place must be given to the rather belated discovery that the childhood and youth of a writer, and especially of a poet, are an essential part of the biographer's subject. It was a discovery not made by the twentieth century, though we have exploited it. The change of perspective implied was forced upon the attention of the nineteenth century by the precocious lives and early deaths of some of its finest poets. The gospel of it all is in Shelley's ' Adonais ', and what is missing in that brief allegory was almost biblically supplied by the ' Prelude ' of Wordsworth. The biography of poets, and presently biography in general, took a new turn. In the eighteenth century, when the biographical form took shape again in Europe, the biographer, whether of poets or of potentates, hastens always to the grown man. All is adult, all is mature. That every poet must go to school, and to a university if he can, and write boyish verses, and fall in love and out of it, all this to Samuel Johnson, the master biographer of the eighteenth century, seemed a trivial and merely normal introduction to the real experiences and trials of life.

We judge these things differently to-day. We have a craving for beginnings, for the seeds of things, for the flower in the bud. It is now, psychology aiding, almost too amply recognized that in those once unnoticed years of youth and childhood every one of us accumulates by far the most valuable part of the

natural riches on which we are to draw for life. On
this fresh capital the poet above all men lives, and
when it is spent, the man may walk, but the poet is
no more. No poet, therefore, who really is a poet,
can ever outlive his youth, and it is merely true that
all good poets die young.

There is an evident danger, of course, that this
discovery may be pushed too far, like the related
discovery which has revolutionized our domestic life,
the discovery that our children have minds and souls
of their own which are entitled to our studious respect.
Biography, in its pursuit of origins, runs the risk of
becoming morbidly and irrelevantly inquisitive. The
lives of some of our poets are already, as I have said,
much better known than their works, and their letters
more often cited than their poems. Our ears are
exercised, not in the still Temple of Urania, but in
the buzz and whisper of the House of Fame, and
' even in still lower traffic, the illicit pleasures of the
keyhole ', while over all the new psychology casts
her darker tinge. These are the shadows of what,
I must think a beneficent change.

THE LITERATURE OF GREEK TRAVEL.

By F. L. Lucas, F.R.S.L.,

Fellow of King's College, Cambridge.

[Read October 13th, 1937.]

Cyriac of Ancona in the fifteenth century, asked by some bewildered contemporary what possessed him to wander in a wilderness of Turks and fleas like Greece, replied, " I go to wake the dead ". That awakening was the Renaissance. Thanks to it the dead of Greece are still awake to watch with their calm marble eyes the frenzies of our fevered world. And yet even to-day every traveller in Greece still needs to waken those dead for himself anew. They are still there. That is why the call of Greeçe is so strong. Perfect travel, for me, demands two qualities in a country—that it shall be full of beauty ; and that it shall be full of ghosts. Lands with too little past may thrill the eye, but not the memory. Yet to make our lives fully living we need also the dead. Now no country is more beautiful in itself than Greece ; none more haunted. And among its phantoms move not only the great figures of its own legend and history, but also that long succession of half-forgotten pilgrims, more varied even than Chaucer's, who have sailed Greek seas and toiled up Greek mountain-sides from Herodotus to Frazer.

That is why I have chosen what may seem a queer

subject. Even a brief and inadequate survey like this may throw a little light from a fresh angle on three different things—on Greece itself, on the art of writing travel-books, and on some characteristic changes in human feeling through two thousand years, from the classical to the medieval and the modern.

It is not generally realized that the Rev. Thomas Cook, that Baptist temperance-missionary who started his famous travel-agency, nearly a century ago, by running special trains for meetings of teetotallers, was descended from Apollo. Religion, temperance, and travel were the interests of both. And not only did the God of Delphi know so much of European geography from Cadiz to the Caucasus that each band of early colonists consulted him before they sailed away ; it was the fame of his oracle that brought the first foreigners to Greece—the envoys of Croesus from Lydia, the two sons of Tarquin (so legend told) from Rome. And from later Rome came the first foreign sight-seers, men like Flamininus the Liberator and Aemilius Paulus who, after breaking Macedon at Pydna, made a regular tour from Delphi to Olympia.

But Rome came not only to see, but to conquer. Already Greece is becoming a land of historic ruins— Corinth, Delos, Mycenae, Sparta, Amphipolis—whose desolation inspires some of the loveliest laments of the 'Anthology '.

" Lost now are the homes of the heroes. Scarce here and
        there a city
    From the dust lifts its head a little, where the sons of the
    gods were born.

And such wert thou, Mycenae, as I passed, a thing of pity—
　Even the goats of the mountain have pastures less
　　forlorn.
The goatherds pointed at thee.　And I heard an old man
　　say—
　' The Giant-builded City, the Golden, here it lay '.
" Where are the towers that crowned thee, the wealth that
　　filled thy portals.
　Thy beauty, Dorian Corinth, whereon men stood to gaze ?
Thy proud dames sprung from Sisyphus, thy shrined
　　Immortals,
　Thy palaces, the myriads that swarmed along thy ways ?
Not a trace, not a trace, unhappy, hast thou left behind in
　　falling—
　All has been seized and ravened by the wild throat of
　　War.
We only, Ocean's children, are still left calling, calling,
　The sea-mews of thy sorrows, along thy lonely shore."

It is the same brooding over glory departed that
inspires the first prose passage in the literature of
Greek travel to become famous—that letter from
Servius Sulpicius consoling Cicero for his daughter's
death, which has become linked for ever with the
memory of Sterne's Uncle Toby.　" ' Where is Troy
and Mycenae, and Thebes and Delos, Persepolis and
Agrigentum,' continued my father, taking up his
book of post-roads which he had laid down.—' What is
become, brother Toby, of Nineveh and Babylon, of
Cizycum and Mitylene ?　The fairest towns that
ever the sun rose upon are no more ;　the names only
are left ;　and those (for many of them are wrong
spelt) are falling themselves by piece-meal to
decay . . .
　" ' Returning out of Asia, when I sailed from
Aegina towards Megara,' (when can this have been,

thought my uncle Toby), ' I began to view the
country round about.—Aegina was behind me, Megara
before, Pyraeus on the right hand, Corinth on the
left.—What flourishing towns now prostrate upon the
earth! Alas! alas! said I to myself, that man
should disturb his soul for the loss of a child, when
so much as this lies awfully buried in his presence!
Remember, said I to myself again,—remember thou
art a man.'

" Now my uncle Toby knew not that this last
paragraph was an extract of Servius Sulpicius'
consolatory letter to Tully:—he had as little skill,
honest man, in the fragments as he had in the whole
pieces of antiquity. . . . 'And pray, brother,'
quoth my uncle Toby, laying the end of his pipe
upon my father's hand, in a kindly way of interruption—but waiting till he finished the account,—
' What year of our Lord was this ? ' ' 'Twas no year
of our Lord,' replied my father. . . . ' That's
impossible,' cried my uncle Toby. . . . ' Simple-
ton ! ' said my father,—' 'Twas forty years before
Christ was born.' "

In this Roman of Cicero's day, nearly two thousand
years before Chateaubriand, it is strange to hear
already the same music of mortality ; so early and so
inevitably even these most classic of ruins took the
sunset colours of romance.

But if Greece was now captive, her conquerors
thronged to her—students like Caesar, Cicero and
Horace ; tourists like Catullus and Virgil, who
caught his fatal malady one burning day among the
ruins of Megara ; exiles like Cicero and those victims
of the Empire who found, like many a Greek Communist

to-day, their St. Helenas in the Cyclades ;   even
Emperors like Augustus, Nero, and Hadrian.

Now that Greece had come to live on and in the
past, guide-books were needed.   We still have fragments of an early one, the so-called pseudo-Dicae-
archus, round about 100 B.C. : *

"Oropus is a nest of cheats, a hive of swindlers,
and nothing could surpass the extortions of its
custom-house officers, whose unconscionable roguery
has from time immemorial become bred in their
very bones. They even charge duty on what is
brought *into* their country. Most of the people are
boors to meet, having long since knocked on the
head the most intelligent among them.   .   .   .

" Thebes, though ancient, is modernly planned,
having been thrice in history destroyed on account of
the surly arrogance of its inhabitants.   It is an
excellent country for horses.   .   .   .   As for the
people, they are spirited and amazingly optimistic,
but headstrong, supercilious, and insulting, quick to
blows and reckless of common justice, alike with
each other and with foreigners.   .   .   .   Accordingly
their lawsuits never last less than thirty years.   Anyone who dares utter a word in public about this
state of affairs, unless he leaves Boeotia in a hurry,
is likely to find himself murdered one dark night
by those whose interest it is that lawsuits *should* go
on.   .   .   .   The women are the prettiest in Greece.
.   .   .   The poet Lacon praises the Boeotians, but
he is lying ; the fact is, he was caught making love
to a Boeotian lady and let off lightly by the injured

---

* C. Müller, ' Fragmenta Historicorum Graecorum ', II, 254 ff. ;
Frazer, ' Pausanias and other Greek Sketches ', 56 ff.

husband. . . . Thence to Anthedon is 160 stadia.
. . . At Thespiae is nothing but pretentiousness
and fine statues."

This puckish unknown is a great contrast to the
serious Strabo, who under Augustus included Greece
in his ' Geography '. But Strabo's acquaintance with
the country was slight ; and an unhappy misdescrip-
tion of Mycenae has convicted him of never having
been there himself. The one outstanding figure in
the ancient literature of Greek travel is his successor
Pausanias.

Pausanias was not a great writer. Like Strabo,
he was not even a Greek, but from Asia Minor. And
Greece, when he wrote her geography (as Plutarch
her last great history) in the second century A.D.,
was a poor shadow of herself. And yet, especially
since Frazer's magnificent edition, Pausanias can be
excellent reading. He is not read enough. He is no
mere Baedeker. He has Plutarch's sense of the
heroic past ; so that when he tells of the repulse of
the Gauls from Thermopylae or the death-struggles
of Messenia, that ancient Poland, a ghost of greatness
rises in him. And he has also, what Plutarch lacked,
a curious streak of romance, when he comes to
tales like those of Coresus and Callirhoe, Argyra
and Selemnus : "For Selemnus was a young shepherd
in the bloom of his years who was loved by Argyra,
the Silver One, a nymph of the sea, who used to
visit him and sleep by his side. But soon his flower
faded and the nymph came back no more. So in his
loneliness he died of love and was changed by Aphrodite into a river. But even when his limbs were
turned to waves, he loved Argyra, as the tale tells

that Alpheius loves Arethusa ; and so Aphrodite
granted him another grace, so that his waters remem-
bered Argyra no more. I have also heard tell that
the stream of Selemnus cures love in man or woman ;
so that if they bathe in it they forget their love. If
there is any truth in the tale, then great riches are
less precious to men than the water of the Selemnus.''
This last sentence sounds cynical ; but Pausanias is
no cynic : ''Pitiful indeed was the fate of the
innocent youths and maidens who perished through
Melanippus and Comaetho ; pitiful too the lot of
their kinsfolk. But the lovers, I hold, escaped
calamity ; for to man alone better it is than life
itself to love and to be loved.'' So with his romantic
stories of the supernatural—the ghosts heard battling
on the midnight plain of Marathon ; the ghost of that
sailor of Odysseus from whom the athlete Euthymus
saved a maiden ; or the sinister shrine of Zeus on
Mount Lycaeus in Arcadia, where human sacrifice
perhaps endured to his own day, and where all
creatures lost their shadows ; so that the hunter
might see his quarry standing there shadowless, yet
dared not pursue it, for whoever entered died within
the year. Pausanias makes such things moving still,
because they moved him. He is a simple man. He
faithfully records, like some medieval pilgrim, the
sacred relics of the ancient world—at Panopeus,
lumps of the clay from which Prometheus made the
first man ; a stuffed merman at Tanagra ; the sceptre
of Agamemnon, the hide of the Calydonian boar,
even the egg of Leda, whence Helen sprang. At
moments we are reminded of Herodotus ; but only
at moments. The genius has departed ; this is not

the first, but the second, childhood of the race.   Soon
there were to be Greek travellers of a different kind ;
little more than a century after Pausanias came
Alaric, to be bathed and banqueted in a trembling
Athens and to leave sacred Eleusis a ruin.

Already the long silence of the Middle Ages is
upon us.   But a fine attempt to recapture what the
tottering Greek Empire still seemed to the barbarian
invader has been made by Kingsley in his ' Ballad of
the Little Baltung ', unhistorical as it is, on the
legendary poisoning of Athanaric by Theodosius and
the vengeance sworn then by the young Alaric.

The Greek Kaiser welcomes his Gothic guest with
smiling perfidy :

> " He showed him his engines of arsmetrick
>   And his wells of quenchless flame,
> And his flying rocks, that guarded his walls
>   From all that against him came.
>
> " He showed him his temples and pillared halls
>   And his streets of houses high ;
> And his watch-towers tall where his star-gazers
>   Sit reading the stars of the sky.
>
> " He showed him ostrich and unicorn,
>   Ape, lion, and tiger keen ;
> And elephants wise roared ' Hail, Kaiser ! '
>   As they had Christians been."

But the Greek Emperor's poison is in the cup of
Athanaric and it is too late to regret the green forests
by the Danube's side.   This same contrast between
the heroic simplicity of the North and the sinister
sophistication of Byzantium recurs still unchanged

half a dozen centuries later, when Viking Scandinavia comes south to " Micklegarth " and the Greek Emperors rally round them that Varangian Guard described by Scott in 'Count Robert of Paris'. Indeed, among our literature of Greek travel may be counted those romantic runes scored in the flank of the stone lion from Piraeus who now sits outside the Arsenal at Venice, and supposed to record a Greek exploit of that Harold Hardrada who was destined to fall one day at Stamford Bridge.*

A similar contrast between warlike West and cunning East recurs two centuries later when the Fourth Crusade floods over Byzantium and fills Greece with that Frankish chivalry whose ruined castles still bring to the land of Achilles the ghost of Lancelot, and whose deeds are told in Lord Rennell of Rodd's ' Princes of Achaia ' and Miller's ' Latins in the Levant '. Those who wonder what the Byzantine Empire looked like to a Crusader's eye will find tantalizing glimpses not only in Villehardouin's Chronicle, but also in the poetry of the Provençal troubadour, Raimbaut de Vaqueiras.†

But now reappear travellers in the ordinary sense. Between 1159 and 1173 the Jew Benjamin of Tudela travelled from Navarre to Bagdad and back. Unfortunately Benjamin was too race-conscious. He is mainly interested in how many other Jews he can find by the way. " Thence in two days you cross to Corfu, which contains but one Jew, a dyer called Joseph." Joseph may have been an excellent dyer,

---

* *Cf.* Snorre Sturlason's account in the ' Heimskringla ' of the deeds at Byzantium of both Harold and King Sigurd the Crusader ; and the curious Byzantine episode which closes ' Grettir's Saga '.

† Edited by Oscar Schultz (1893).

but he is not exactly the one thing we should choose to
hear about in twelfth-century Corfu. But Benjamin
plods on to find 50 Jews at Patras, 100 at Lepanto,
200 on Parnassus, 300 at Corinth, and no less than
5000 in the fortunate city of Thebes. He is more
interesting about the Vlachs, those nomad shepherds
still familiar to the Greek traveller of to-day : " They
are nimble as deer and from their mountains descend
robbing and raiding into the plains of Greece. None
dares make war on them and no king can subdue
them ; and they are not Christians." Anyone who
has dealt with their dogs will agree.

The next visitor known to me after Benjamin of
Tudela is the Englishman, John of Basingstoke,
Archdeacon of Leicester in the thirteenth century.
He records that he had learnt less from all the doctors
of Paris than from a certain young lady of Athens,
Constantina, daughter of the Archbishop, who in
her teens was already mistress of the Seven Arts
and could predict eclipses, earthquakes, storms and
plagues. Unfortunately the contemporary Archbishop of Athens, Akominatos, disclaims having any
children. We are left to weigh the word of a Greek
Archbishop against that of an English Archdeacon.
But at least it appears that some relics of culture
still lived in thirteenth-century Athens.

The fourteenth brings us to a more entertaining
traveller, Sir John Mandeville, whose work is even
more of a traveller's tale than most. First, it is not
by Sir John Mandeville ; secondly, its compiler, a
Belgian physician of Liège, seems to have travelled
mainly from shelf to shelf of his library. Being
about as veracious as Othello's tales to Desdemona

of men with heads beneath their shoulders, his book enjoyed a wild success. The Greek section is brief ; but it tells with vivid touches of Justinian's statue in Byzantium, whose hand now refused to hold the magic apple long since fallen from it and betokening his empire's lost provinces ; and of Mount Athos (he should have said Olympus, but miscopied what he stole), who casts his shadow 76 miles and has a summit so dry that certain wise philosophers, climbing it with sponges to their noses, found still unchanged the letters they had traced there in the snow a year before. He tells too of the Isle of Cos, where "is yit the doughter of Ypocras, in forme and lykness of a gret dragoun that is an hundred fadme in lengthe as men seyn, for" (a characteristically perfidious touch) "I haue not seen hire". The unhappy lady had been thus afflicted by Diana ; and a dragon she was doomed to remain until kissed by a knight. Attempts had been made by various bold gentlemen ; but their hearts always failed at the supreme moment. "And whan the knyght saugh hire in that forme so hidous and so horrible he fleygh away and the dragoun bare the knyght vpon a rocke mawgree his hede. And from that rocke sche caste him in to the see." This typical medieval jumble seems ultimately derived from the story of Diana and Callisto, from the sacred snake of Asclepios, and from the fact that Hippocrates had a son, or grandson, called Draco. But how much the world would have lost if the Middle Ages had been scientific !

Niccolò de Martini, a notary of Capua, who really did visit Athens at the end of the fourteenth century, found there not one inn and only a thousand houses.

But he eagerly records how there used to be an idol in an iron-bound cave above the Theatre, which sank hostile ships as soon as they crossed the horizon— a far-off memory, doubtless, of the Gorgon's head which Pausanias describes on the Acropolis.

With our next traveller, the Florentine Buondelmonti, we can see the medieval idea of Greece as a land of sinister magic beginning to yield to the Renaissance sense of its departed glory. Early in the fifteenth century, while Henry V was conquering France, Buondelmonti visited Rhodes and the islands. He is still a credulous soul ; he too tells of the daughter of Hippocrates in Cos. Yet there is a change. He comes to study Greek ; and at Delos he and his companions, finding the great Apollo of the Naxians prostrate on the shore, have the new idea of trying to set it on its legs again. " But with all the machines and tackling of our galleys we could not, though we were more than a thousand." Thera proved more perilous. " Being in these parts on board a Genoese vessel we saw an octopus sixty cubits in compass, stretching forth his tentacles and advancing upon us. In panic we left our ship and hurried on shore, where from higher ground we could contemplate the monster. Soon however a fair wind swelled our canvas and joyfully we sailed away."

Cyriac of Ancona is still more of a Renaissance figure. Like Schliemann, a self-taught merchant with a passion for antiquity, he wandered all over Italy and the Levant, now hunting with the Greek Emperor, now employed as Greek reader by Mahomet II at the siege of Constantinople. Returning from

Greece, we are told, when eighty miles on his way he heard of an inscription he had missed, and back he went. He was inaccurate and uncritical ; he imagined he had found Homer's grave in Chios " by the roots of an old fig-tree " ; there are faults in his Latin verses ; he sometimes miscopied his inscriptions; he was even accused of forging them. But let him be forgiven—*quia multum amavit*. We see him like a great bumble-bee, drunk with the honey of antiquity, humming in wide tireless circles about the Levant. A typical passage tells how a giant Spartan carried him across the Eurotas, then snapped in his hands a bar of iron : in celebration, the delighted Cyriac composed a sonnet.

Constantinople fell. Five years later in 1458 Athens was visited by Mahomet II in person, anxious to see " the mother of the philosophers "—" dearest of the cities of his empire ". (We must remember that Plato himself left his mark on the Ottoman constitution, with its system of Janissaries.) There still exists a Greek guide of the period, perhaps composed for the Sultan's use. Accuracy is not its greatest charm. It describes the tiny temple of Nike on the Acropolis as " a small school of musicians, founded by Pythagoras ". They must have been very small musicians.

Then, after Sigismondo Malatesta in 1463 had carried back from Sparta to Rimini the bones of Gemistos Plethon, that last star of Byzantine learning, with the later Renaissance there comes a gap. The Turkish conquest must have proved a barrier : in conflict with it at Lepanto, near where Byron was to lose his life, Cervantes lost his hand. But in the early seventeenth century the Greek hills saw one of the queerest of all their travellers, Thomas Coryate.

Coryate of Odcombe in Somerset, once a buffoon of Prince Henry's, won a grotesque fame by his ' Coryate's Crudities ', describing how he walked 2000 miles in five months; half of the way in one pair of shoes, which hung gloriously for a century after in Odcombe Church.

He had a head like a sugar-loaf, says Anthony à Wood, and " a very coveting eye, that could never be satisfied with seeing ".   In 1612, after a farewell oration to the citizens of Odcombe, he set out on a new ten years' walk by Greece and Egypt into India ; five years later he died at Surat of the over-generous hospitality of the English merchants there.   He has not much to say of Greece proper ; but his description of Troy makes extraordinary reading.*   He arrived with fourteen other English and " a Jew or Drugger-man ".   After they had wandered round the ruins, identifying Priam's tomb and the like to Coryate's satisfaction, his companion Robert Rugge, whipping out his sword and reciting some extempore doggerel, dubbed Coryate " the first English knight of Troy " —much to the alarm of their two Turkish guides, who thought a murder was in progress.   Coryate replied in more doggerel, their musketeers fired two volleys in rejoicing, and our hero then delivered an equally ridiculous oration on previous visitors to Troy, from Achilles to Caracalla, and on the solemn warning its fate afforded against adultery.

At the same period Scotland produced a rival

* ' Master T. Coryate's Travels to and Observations in Constantinople and Other Places ' (printed in the 1776 edition of the ' Crudities ').

eccentric in William Lithgow of Lanark, whose
' Totall Discourse of the Rare Adventures and
painefull Peregrinations of long nineteene Yeares
Travaylles' (1632) claims that he covered on his
" paynefull feet " over 36,000 miles. Greece he *says*
he traversed in 1609. But his ideas of Greek topo-
graphy and English prose are equally peculiar.
"Athens," he says, " is still inhabited, standing in
the East part of Peloponnesus, neere to the frontiers
of Macedon, or Thessaly by the Seaside." " Thessaly
. . . lieth betweene Peloponnesus and Achaia :
Wherein standeth the hill Olympus, on which Hercules
did institute the Olympian games." Sailing east
from Salonika, he had the good fortune to find
Parnassus several hundred miles out of its usual
place. It had " two toppes, the one whereof is
dry, and sandy, signifying that Poets are always
poore, and needy : the other top is barren, and rocky,
resembling the ingratitude of wretched and niggardly
Patrons."

He grows eloquent over his hardships: " But this
I remember, amongst these rockes my belly was
perished, and wearied was my body, with the climbing
of fastidious mountains." On ship it was as bad:
" Between Serigo and Carebusa we had sevenscore
and twelve miles of dangerous and combustious seas."
Even a fastidious mountain must have been better
than a combustious sea.

And yet there is a sort of Tom o' Bedlam lilt about
his prose, with its blending of the Old Testament
and Ancient Pistol: " Here in Argos I had the
ground to be a pillow, and the world-wide fields to
be a chamber, the whirling windy skies to be a roof

to my Winter-blasted lodging, and the humide
vapours of cold Nocturna to accompany the unwished-
for bed of my repose." However he consoled himself
on this painful occasion by composing a satire on
women, inspired by the memory of Helen.

Lithgow repays his reader; though a man who
tells us he saw at Rome, in "the Library of the
auncient Romans", "the Saphicke verses of that
Lesbian Sappho" with many other ancient authors,
"all wrote with their owne hands, and sealed with
their names, and manuall subscriptions", must rank
high in the calendar of unblushing liars.

But two more serious travellers await us—that
entente cordiale, Monsieur Jacob Spon and Mr. George
Wheler. Spon (1647–85), a Protestant of Lyons and
doctor by profession, had all the antiquarian passion
of Cyriac: "C'est mon feu, c'est ma passion que les
inscriptions antiques." In 1675 he found himself
alone in Rome, his companion Vaillant having been
carried off on his way from Marseilles by an Algerian
corsair; he met Wheler, botanist and antiquarian,
and together they set out for Greece. Spon returned
loaded with manuscripts and copies of inscriptions;
and his ' Voyage ' (1678) is the first serious account of
Greek monuments. But he lost his patients, who
thought so good an archaeologist must be a very
bad doctor and too likely to provide them with
funeral monuments of their own; and when he
dedicated his book to Père La Chaise, Louis XIV's
confessor, the father merely recommended him to turn
Catholic. Spon wrote, and published, a too boldly
Protestant reply, which ended in his flight to Switzer-
land and untimely death at Vevey.

But Spon, though a deeper scholar, is less readable than his English companion, who in 1682 dedicated to Charles II his ' Journey into Greece ', courteously adding Spon's name on his title-page, just as Spon had added *his*.   More fortunate, too, than Spon, he was knighted, took orders, and only died in 1723, after producing eighteen children and another work, clearly inspired by them—' The Protestant Monastery : or Christian Oeconomicks, containing Directions for the Religious Conduct of a Family'.

But his account of Greece is delightful.   For him, fortunate man, the Parthenon was intact ;   the Turks proved not too Turkish ; and there were no tourists. He is admirable at describing, with a mixture of sly humour and simplicity, his adventure marooned on Delos ; or the wicked " Haga " of Athens who planned to blow up the church of St. Demetrios and was hoist by that saint with his own petard (though, alas, the Propylaea flew skyward with him) ; or the Mainote village where the old woman of the house, asked by some travellers she was lodging why she was weeping and tearing her hair, replied, " Because my son is not at home to rob you " ; or the " extream civil " pirates of Myconos ; or the old hermit whom Wheler met and envied at St. Luke's in Stiris under the quiet shadow of Helicon.

A storm at sea even inspires him to versify a psalm, with results less happy :

" The Waves lift up their voice, the Billows rage :
  No Mortal Pow'r their Fury can asswage.
  They foam and roar ; they toss the Ships so high,
  That many times they seem to touch the Skie :

> Few there have any appetite to Meat ;
> And those that have, can nowhere sit to eat.
> Like Drunken Men they stagger to and fro :
> On dancing Decks what mortal Man can go ? "

But his prose is very endearing : witness this picture of Achaea under the Turks. In the mountains he comes on thirty or forty shepherds " sitting in a round heap together. This made me presently call to mind the pleasant stories I had heard of the *Arcadian* Shepherds, from whose Country we were now not far distant :· I thought of nothing, but being diverted by some Festival, some Sport or other among them ; or, at least, that there had been the Nuptials of some fair Shepherdess then celebrated. . . . But approaching nearer, I was soon undeceived ; finding an old Grey-bearded Turk, sitting in the middle of the Circle, like a Conjurer, with his Lap full of Pebles, Pen, Ink, and Paper by him, and giving each of them their Task ; which was to turn five of those stones into so many Dollers by the next day at that time, upon pain of being made Slaves, and sent to the Gallies, if they failed. . . . The number of Pebles that were then to be made Dollers, was Four hundred and thirteen ; by a People, that I dare engage, knew nothing of the *Philosopher's Stone.*"

From now on the stream of Greek travellers thickens fast. There is no time, alas, to dwell even on curious figures like Guillet de St. Georges, who produced a book on Athens in 1675 without ever going there ; and, being exposed by Spon, brazenly accused his accuser of not having been there himself. But he is an amusing rogue ; as when he describes a

Turkish dinner where he and his companions, busy
staring at the lattice concealing their host's harem,
found the servants had slyly replaced the plates
they were eating from by others containing "Coleworts
and Turneps and little Kitlings newly born", which
they put without noticing in their mouths. Nor is
there space here for the admirable botanist Tourne-
fort, or that queer maniac the Abbé Fourmont, sent
by Louis XV to the Levant in 1729, who after copying
his inscriptions smashed them. "Depuis plus de
trente jours," he writes triumphant home, "trente
et quelquefois quarante ou soixante ouvriers abat-
tent, détruisent, exterminent la ville de Sparte.   . . .
Imaginez-vous, si vous pouvez, dans quelle joie je
suis.   . . . Sparte est la cinquième ville de Morée
que j'ai renversée." Fortunately the Abbé seems to
have been mendacious as well as mad and to have
wrought little of the havoc that he claims.

Nor can we deal here with the worthy Chandler,
who so delightfully describes the Dervishes dancing
in the Tower of the Winds at Athens, or the careful
and sober Leake, or the admirable Pouqueville who
had served under Napoleon and negotiated with
Nelson in Egypt before he found himself a Turkish
prisoner in the Morea. It is time to turn to those
two supreme Greek travellers—Chateaubriand and
Byron.

Chateaubriand's ' Itinéraire de Paris à Jérusalem ',
despite its lapses from sublime to ridiculous, is still
unsurpassed. A great, though exasperating personality ; a great subject ; a great style—these three
do not often meet in one.

He travelled in 1806 and published in 1811. The

motives of his journey were three, as he admitted at
different times.   First, he sought colour and imagery
for his prose epic of Christianity, ' Les Martyrs '.
Secondly he saw himself as " The Last of the Pilgrims "—" I shall perhaps be the last Frenchman to
visit the Holy Land in the pilgrim spirit of old."
He was, that is, a follower of Joinville in the cynical
age of Talleyrand.   Thirdly and incongruously
enough, this romantic pilgrimage was to conclude
with a romantic assignation at the Alhambra in
Spain with Natalie de Noailles, Mme. de Mouchy.
Few champions of Christianity have ever been as
pagan as Chateaubriand ;   the main tenet in his
creed was really " I will have no other God but
me ".

In the end the Pilgrim duly arrived in the Alhambra,
but, alas, two months late : and Mme. de Mouchy was
no Penelope.   " I am an unfortunate woman," she
once said ;   " no sooner do I fall in love with one man
than I meet another I like better."   And so at the
Alhambra Mme. de Mouchy was in black and in
tears ;   she had met a most charming colonel—and
then he had died.   However, Chateaubriand succeeded
in consoling her.   Yet tragedy crept into the comedy,
when Mme. de Mouchy grew jealous of the Duchesse
de Duras and during the Hundred Days at last went
mad.   It is well to feel all this in the ironic background
as one reads Chateaubriand's book.

It remains one of his best.   There is more than
usual of that charming smile of his, which he denied
to his sombre René ;   and less stilted solemnity, less
brooding on his bored ego.   Travel shook up Chateaubriand ;   and he needed shaking.

The work is not very learned, though not always above pretending to be. But he loathed libraries—those " nids de rats ". And he scandalized Dr. Avramiotti at Argos by just galloping up a hill for an eagle's-eye view, instead of conscientiously poring over the sites. But after all there are a thousand scholars for one poet like Chateaubriand. He has that strange Circe's wand which can transform even foolish creatures back into God's image—style.

Hence he must be read in full : he cannot be conveyed in summary. The reader must be lulled—except when some crowning absurdity breaks the spell, not unpleasantly, with a sudden gust of laughter—by the long roll of those melancholy sentences with which Chateaubriand first taught French to equal the surge of the English Bible or the organ-march of Sir Thomas Browne.

Sailing from Venice, by Corfu and Ithaca, he landed at Modon in Messenia. " Pas un bateau dans le port, pas un homme sur la rive : partout le silence, l'abandon et l'oubli." Then enter bands of Janissaries and Turks. The roads proved for the moment unusually clear of brigands : for the Pasha of the Morea had just cleared up the district of Mount Ithome by the simple method of drawing a cordon round and killing all within it. It is true that this cost also the lives of three hundred innocent peasants. One might be in modern Abyssinia.

The cavalcade sets out : first, the guide with a spare horse, then an armed Janissary, then Chateaubriand also armed, and at the rear his Milanese valet, Joseph, a little fair, fat man sweltering in blue velvet through a Greek August. Each evening they

reach an empty "khan" or inn; the Janissary
goes out to hunt a fowl, which Chateaubriand insists
on paying for; they eat with their fingers, wash
them in the brook, then sleep on the floor "parmi
toutes sortes d'insectes et de reptiles". "Voilà
comme on voyage aujourd'hui dans le pays d'Alcibiade
et d'Aspasie."

Sometimes things are even worse, as at the approach
to Sparta, where the khan is occupied by an old
Turk squatted among goats and goat-droppings:
"J'avais mangé l'ours et le chien sacré avec les
Sauvages; je partageai depuis le repas des Bédouins;
mais je n'ai jamais rien rencontré de comparable à ce
premier kan de la Laconie." Sometimes things are
better: "Il y même à Misitra une maison grecque
qu'on appelle *l'Auberge anglaise*: on y mange du
roast-beef, et l'on y boit du vin de Porto. Le
voyageur a sous ce rapport de grandes obligations
aux Anglais: ce sont eux qui ont établi de bonnes
auberges dans toute l'Europe . . . jusqu'aux
portes de Sparte, en dépit de Lycurgue."

True, the little Spartans of Mistra amused themselves by pushing pieces of the ruins on top of him;
but there was the consolation of finding there his own
'Atala' translated into modern Greek. What more
could author desire? Then comes one of the sub-
limely absurd moments. With difficulty he finds his
way to the site of Sparta. The sun is just rising over
the range of Menelaïon amid the silence of the ruins:
"Je criai de toute ma force: Léonidas! Aucune
ruine ne répéta ce grand nom, et Sparte même sembla
l'avoir oublié."

And yet a moment later the magic returns; as

on the surface of a woodland-pool the ripples of some stone dropped in disappear and the mirrored forest stands dreaming there again. He sees some blue lilies on an islet in the Eurotas—"j'en cueillis plusieurs, en mémoire d'Hélène ; la fragile couronne de la beauté existe encore sur les bords de l'Eurotas, et la beauté même a disparu."

He crosses Mount Parthenius, loses himself and catches a fever in the legendary marshes of Lerna, is led by a naked shepherd-boy to the tomb of Aga-memnon and the ruins of Mycenae. Corinth produces a typical and comical flourish of grandiloquence : "Je ne parle point de Denys et de Timoléon. . . . Si jamais je montais sur un trône, je n'en descendrais que mort ; et je ne serai jamais assez vertueux pour tuer mon frère ; je ne me soucie donc point de ces deux hommes."

Beyond the Isthmus a Turkish commandant demon-strated to the Frankish stranger the excellence of his carbine by casually sniping a peaceful peasant on the neighbouring hill ; the wretch crawled in, wounded and weeping, and was given fifty stripes by way of compensation.

So at last Chateaubriand arrived in an Athens whose Piraeus showed not a single sail and only a single wooden shed for its Turk douanier : nothing now but the cry of wave and sea-bird by the grave of Themistocles. With a last description of dawn on the Acropolis we will leave Chateaubriand to sail on under Sunium for his Holy Land : "J'ai vu, du haut de l'Acropolis, le soleil se lever entre les deux cimes du mont Hymette : " (it has not two summits ; but no matter) : "les corneilles qui nichent autour

de la citadelle, mais qui ne franchissent jamais son
sommet, planaient au-dessous de nous ; leur ailes
noires et lustrées étaient glacées de rose par les
premiers reflets du jour. . . . Athènes, l'Acropolis, et les débris du Parthénon se coloraient de la
plus belle teinte de la fleur du pêcher ; les sculptures
de Phidias, frappées horizontalement d'un rayon
d'or, s'animaient, et semblaient se mouvoir sur le
marbre par la mobilité des ombres du relief ; au
loin, la mer et le Pirée étaient tout blancs de lumière ;
et la citadelle de Corinthe, renvoyant l'éclat du jour
nouveau, brillait sur l'horizon du couchant, comme
un rocher de pourpre et de feu."

Three years later, in 1809, Childe Harold left
England on *his* pilgrimage. By way of Lisbon and
Malta he arrived in Albania and at Janina visited
Ali Pasha, now a little plump man of seventy, who
in his time had roasted enemies alive and drowned a
dozen women to humour a daughter-in-law. He
liked Byron and praised the breeding of Byron's
small ears and little white hands ; while Byron was
ravished by all this and by "the glittering minarets
of Tepalen " with their feudal pageantry that
reminded him of Scott's Branksome Castle. At
Janina he began ' Childe Harold '. But Byron's
poem lacks the perfection—and the poetry—of
Chateaubriand's prose. Most moderns will prefer
Byron's letters with their Sancho Panzan picture of
his valet, Fletcher ; who, poor man, after the
terrors of a fearful storm in the Albanian hills found
himself facing still worse terrors at sea. " Fletcher
yelled after his wife, the Greeks called on all the
saints, the Mussulmans on Allah ; the captain burst

into tears." After trying to console Fletcher, who could only moan about "a watery grave", Byron calmly lay down in his cloak on deck; and was delighted to be driven ashore at 1 a.m. among the picturesque cut-throats of Suli.

Like Chateaubriand, Byron was scornful of archaeological fervour. His companion Hobhouse, he says, "would potter with map and compass at the foot of Pindus, Parnes, and Parnassus, to ascertain the site of some ancient temple or city. I rode my mule up them. They haunted my dreams from boyhood; the pines, eagles, vultures and owls were descended from those that Themistocles and Alexander had seen, and were not degenerated like the humans."

The trio arrives at Athens. "Ah, my Lord," cried Fletcher on the Acropolis, "what chimney-pieces one could make with all this marble!" "Magnificent!" exclaimed Hobhouse surveying the Parthenon. "Very like the Mansion House," said Byron. But that did not prevent him from trouncing in both prose and verse the vandalism of Lord Elgin, then busily at work.

They took rooms in Athens; Byron in the house of a widow with three fair daughters, all under fifteen, Theresa, Mariana, Katinka. It was for Theresa that he wrote:

> "Maid of Athens, ere we part,
> Give, oh give me back my heart . . .
> Hear my vow, before I go,
> Ζώη μοῦ, σὰς ἀγαπῶ.

Perhaps too it was for her that he wounded his own breast with a dagger, in the fashion of Eastern lovers, while the lady looked coldly on. But (alas for romance) in the end poor Theresa married a Mr. Black and died at eighty, penniless.

After being nearly waylaid by some Mainotes at Sunium, Byron and Hobhouse sailed for the Helles-pont, where Byron performed that feat he valued beyond all he had ever done, by swimming from Sestos to Abydos : and so to the Bosphorus where, perched on the Symplegades, he scribbled his parody of the ' Medea ' :

> " Oh, how I wish that an embargo
> Had kept in port the good ship Argo ! "

Returned for a second stay to Athens, he lodged for a time in the Choragic Monument of Lysicrates, then part of a Capucin monastery, busy teaching the Abbot's pupils to box or rescuing young ladies on their way to be thrown into the sea in a sack ; while even Fletcher, after all his complaints of the lack of beer, beef and tea, of resin in the wines and bugs in the beds, now consoled himself for the young bride he had left in England with an Athenian Circe.

There followed a second trip to the Morea, which enabled Fletcher to put his foot in a boiling kettle at Megara. At Patras Byron nearly died of fever, while Fletcher and the doctor both lost their heads. But Byron's Albanian servants swore to kill the doctor if their master died, the doctor wisely fled, and Byron recovered for fourteen years more.

I have recalled enough to send readers back to the strong and astringent letters in which Byron records these things. With his tragic return to Greece I

need not deal. It belongs not so much to Greek
travel as to the history of Europe. But one moment
in it is worth reviving here. They were approaching
Cephalonia ; the plaintive but faithful Fletcher was
still there: "My master," he confided, Sancho-
like, to Trelawny, "can't be right in his mind.
Why, sir, there is nothing to eat in Greece, or to
drink ; there is nothing but rocks, robbers, and
vermin. I defy my Lord to deny it."

Byron overheard : " I don't deny it. What he
says is quite true to those who take a hog's eye view
of things. But this I know, I was never so happy as
when I was there."

It was true, I believe, for him as for many another
Greek traveller. And to Byron life and death were
kinder in Greece than in England. The tragedy of
Missolonghi was his finest poem. And next to it
may stand that part of his ' Don Juan ' which tells
of the love of Juan and Haidee among the Cyclades,
and embodies those lines which, even though England
has forgotten now the spirit of Navarino, will outlive
the Dictators of to-day, who of their grace and wisdom
tell us we are tired of liberty :

> " The mountains look on Marathon
>   And Marathon looks on the sea,
> And musing there an hour alone
>   I dreamed that Greece might yet be free.
> For standing on the Persian's grave
> I could not deem myself a slave."

We have far from exhausted the pageant of Greek
travellers. We must leave Byron's own friends,

Hobhouse, and Galt, and that old pirate Trelawny, who came with him to fight for Greece and outraged his friend's corpse and married a whole seraglio, including the daughter of the Greek bandit Odysseus, and sat six weeks motionless in the cave on Parnassus where a traitor had shot him in the back, and yet was eighty-nine before he was laid at last by Shelley in the Protestant Cemetery at Rome ; and Christopher Wordsworth, the poet's nephew, who came to Athens in 1832, when it was unsafe to stir beyond the walls and there were no newspapers, while letters were cried in the streets and burnt if unclaimed ; and Dodwell, whose *camera obscura* spread consternation among the Turks on the Acropolis, lest he should put them bodily in his " magic box " and carry them away ; and Edward Lear, who also painted Greece and had a poem written on his travels by Tennyson ; and Lamartine, who is watery and disappointing ; and Edmond About, whose impish ' Roi des Montagnes ' gave many of us at school our first picture of Greek brigands ; and Flaubert, returning from Egypt ; and Heinrich Schliemann, whose simple faith raised to life again the dead of Troy, Tiryns, and Mycenae ; and the sensitive pen of Sir James Frazer in our own day.

But I have said enough to suggest how happily one can travel through Greece in one's head, as well as on one's feet. True, Greek travel has produced no work quite so famous as Johnson's ' Hebrides ' or Doughty's 'Arabia '. It hardly will now : for to-day even Greece begins to be vulgarized. But in the pages of Pausanias, of Wheler, of Chateaubriand, of Byron, we can revisit an older Greece, dead now, yet

safe for ever from the grinding march of the machine,
in that Universe of Ideas where—

> " Another Peneus rolls his fountains
>   Against the morning star,"

with no railroad through Tempe at his side.   To-day
we no longer hitch our wagons to stars.   We have
all bought automobiles :   and our stars have sunk
reddening westward to Hollywood.   Published to-day,
Chateaubriand would be giggled at, Byron silenced
with jeers of " Rhetoric ! "   It may even be that,
neglected in a world of mechanism and brutality,
those Greek dead whom Cyriac of Ancona went
long since to waken, may die for a while a second
death.   But, for the present, the Greek past is still
ours :   and this sketch may help a few readers, above
all those who have had the good fortune to tread
Greek soil themselves, to forget, for a moment, the
poisoned vapours of the present in that clearer and
cleaner air.

MARIGOLD OF THE POETS.

By Professor Leslie Hotson, Ph.D., F.R.S.L.

[Read June 1st, 1938.]

If the title of my paper has an enigmatic sound, that is as it should be, for the rare Elizabethan poem which it considers is a puzzle. I need not apologize to anyone who has been charmed by the daily cross-word for presenting a minor literary conundrum. And I shall offer nothing so dull, I hope, as a complete solution of all its fascinating problems. Indeed, after my best efforts have been spent on its mysteries, the central enigma, as in the case of Shakespeare's sonnets, remains. Still, the adventure of untying some of its knots has not only been delightful in itself, but has produced interesting discoveries by the way, and has taken me into very lively company. You will hear of a phantom author introduced into the ' Dictionary of National Biography '; of a lost poem whose reading, in the home circle of an Elizabethan county family, was made a matter for the Star Chamber; of another poem—the Marigold itself—which the Archbishop of Canterbury ordered to be burnt, but which was not burnt. You will also hear of a certain letter of dangerous contents : the Queen's Champion wrote it, a leading Elizabethan poet was told to burn it, but instead concealed it in a wall ; a tyrannical earl tore down the wall, got it out, and was so infuriated with what he read in it about himself that he brought an action against the Champion for *scandalum magnatum*.

In short, when the scattered limbs of the story are brought together we shall have another proof of the fact that in Shakespeare's lifetime feuds were fostered as well by the pen as by the sword ; that poems were close to poniards, rhymes to rapiers, and quatrains to quarrels.

But to go back to the beginning of my tale. On the 1st of July, 1599, the Archbishop of Canterbury joined with the Bishop of London in sending a command to the Stationers' Company. The copies of certain objectionable books of satires and epigrams and licentious poetry were to be burnt. Among the proscribed are numbered Hall's satires, Marston's ' Pygmalion ' and his ' Scourge of Villainy ', Middleton's ' Snarling Satires ', Davies's ' Epigrams ', Marlowe's translation of Ovid's ' Elegies '. These, of course, are well known. Fortunately they were already in circulation, and so not all the copies of them fed the sacrificial fire in Stationers' Hall.

Now it is in this list of condemned books that we find the title ' Caltha Poetarum ', which we may translate as the Marigold (or Marsh-marigold) of the Poets. It had been entered at Stationers' Hall only two months earlier. On the day of burning, for some unknown reason, ' Caltha ' was not flung to the flames, but ordered by the Master and Wardens of the Company to be " stayed ".

Who wrote this *rarissima* which Whitgift found so damnable ? The bibliographers give the author's name as T. Cutwode. I confess that this name sounded un-English to me, and I suspected its *bona fides* from the first. My suspicion, and it must be admitted, a curiosity to learn what made the Archbishop condemn the book, drove me to the British Museum to see for myself. The volume proved to be a tiny octavo—so small that when I called for it at the North Library desk the assistant had difficulty in finding the little thing, where it was hiding beside a bookrack.

Opening it we discover the owner's stamp of George Steevens, and an inserted inscription : " To my dear Father—This Copy of one of the Rarest Pieces of English Poetry, & a not inelegant Specimen of the Literature of the Elizabethan Period, is presented by his grateful & affectionate H. Freeling. Christmas Eve 1833." The title-page announces ' Caltha Poetarum, or the Bumble Bee ', and carries a large woodcut of a bee. The author's name is given as T. Cutwode, Esq. That addition of esquire, which in Elizabethan times meant social position and the possession of a coat of arms, deepened my suspicions. Among the thousands of Elizabethan names which have passed under my eyes in the last fifteen years, there has never been a man of any rank by the name of Cutwode. But in a moment we find a further clue in the verses of a certain G.S. in commendation of the author :

> Admire his skill and choyce conceit most purely prest,
> From homebred soyle and *Nature* he it hither brings,
> By birth from noble progeny (lo) thus he sings.

The self-styled " Cutwode ", then, is announced by his friend as " by birth from *noble* progeny ".

Curiouser and curiouser. Cutwode is not a name borne by any English noble family.

But we have not far to seek. The author gives us the final hint of his identity in stanza 5 of his poem :

> There is a Citie lying neare the North,
>   By name ycleapéd *Nycol* heretofore,
> Where ancient *Lacyes* men of mickle worth,
>   were Rulers many a hundreth yeares of yore,
> And domineered with dignitie and power.
> Thy Earldome (*Nycol*) then did bear great sway,
> But Earldoms, Earles, & Counties now decay.

Here at last is something tangible. *Nycol*, the northern city ruled of old by the Lacys, is of course Lincoln. The ancient state of Lincoln calls to mind the timeworn prophecy, " Lincoln was, London is, and York shall be ". This oracle inspired Thomas Fuller, in his ' Worthies ', to remark " That Lincoln was namely a fairer, greater, richer city . . . doth plainly appear by the ruines thereof . . . That London is, we know ; that York shall be, God knows." Perhaps Fuller spoke too soon. Surely the nameless seer, when he declared that York shall be, had his prophetic eye on *New* York.

At all events we now have definite information in hand. Lincoln is the scene of the poem ; the author is an esquire " by birth from noble progeny ", who calls himself Cutwode, and who as we have seen casts a slight upon the contemporary Earl of Lincoln in the couplet :

> Thy Earldome (*Nycol*) then did bear great sway,
> But Earldoms, Earles, & Counties now decay.

Now it is common knowledge that the storm-centre

of trouble in Lincolnshire at this period was Henry, 2nd Earl of Lincoln, a man whose tyranny and violence were so unbridled as to raise a doubt of his sanity. It is also well known that he carried on a bitter feud for many years with his nephew, Sir Edward Dymoke, the Queen's Champion. Just four years ago, in his excellent book, ' Godes Peace and the Queenes ', Mr. Norreys O'Conor added to our knowledge the story of how a brother of the Champion, living with Sir Edward, and named Tailboys Dymoke, wrote and produced a May-games play and a mock sermon to bait their detestable uncle the Earl.

And here, in the spirited and satirical Tailboys Dymoke, whom his uncle denounced as " a common contriver and publisher of infamous pamphlets and libels ", I think we have run the mysterious Cutwode, the author of ' Caltha Poetarum ', to earth. What is Tailboys but *Taille-bois* or Cut-wood ? Surtees assures us that the noble name Tailboys " is evidently a personal appellative, like *Taille-fer*, and from some feat of personal strength ". Tailboys Dymoke, like Cutwode, was " by birth from noble progeny ". Anne Tailboys, his father's mother, was daughter to one Lord Tailboys of Kyme, and his maternal grand-mother was the widow of another.

A confirmation of the identity of Cutwode and Tailboys Dymoke is furnished in the opening stanza of the ' Marigold of the Poets '. We have been warned by G.S. that Cutwode is presenting a personal allegory :

> Without offence or fault, by Flower, Plant, or Tree,
> Persons of good worth are meant, conceale thus doth hee.

Beginning his poem by describing a garden, the author
mentions the Red Rose and the White, " whence
comes our kings and queens of Regall Race ", the
Flower de Luce, the Pansies, " who represents a
geanalog of kings ".   He then proceeds to an allegory
or dark conceit of his own family the Dymokes, the
hereditary Champions who receive a cup from their
sovereign's hands at the successive coronations :

> By them do grow the kingcups like to gold,
>   with sops in wine, that every heart delights :
> Which cups the Kings in compliments do hold,
>   carousing to their champions & their knights :
> That in their service, for their honor fights :
> Kissing the cup, and drinking to the health
> Both of their kings, & of their Commonwealth.

This is unmistakable.   And when we recall from
Mr. O'Conor's book the statement that the cognizance,
badge, or device both of the town of Kyme and of
Tailboys Dymoke was a bull, the next stanza gives
up its meaning :

> Next growes the blew cornuted Collumbine
>   like to the crooked hornes of *Acheloy*
> When he in shape and Metamorphosin
>   of mightie Bull, the wrastler did annoy,
> But yet the striver did this beast destroy :
> And when this monstrous battle did surceace,
> His hornes became our threaserhouse of peace.

So far, good.   I think we may be confident that in
this poem of Lincoln, with its slur on the vexatious
earl, its praise of the champions and their king-cups,
and its celebration of the bull, we have a work by that
sprout from a noble stock Tailboys Dymoke.   No

doubt he has himself to blame that a spectral Cutwode masquerades in his room in the ' Dictionary of National Biography ' ; but there can now be no reason to carry on the innocent fiction.

On reaching this point in my inquiry into the ' Marigold of the Poets ' I reflected that it was in the records of suits in the Star Chamber that Mr. O'Conor had found Tailboys Dymoke. It was there that his jocular May-games play was painted in such lively colours ; there that his enraged uncle Lord Lincoln had called him a " common contriver of infamous pamphlets and libels ". It occurred to me that the judicial records might shed further light on his literary activities, and I betook myself to the Record Office. Seldom is the patient seeker sent quite empty away ; and my reward was the discovery of an earlier suit brought by the earl against Tailboys and others of the Dymoke family. The 'Marigold', as we have seen, dates from 1599, the May-games play from 1601 ; but in this new litigation we are taken back to the autumn of 1590. Once again the earl's accusation is that the Dymokes have set forth a slanderous pamphlet against him and his relations, as he says, " against their persons, arms, badges, cognizances " ; and that therein they " have designed and noted " him " by his cognizance and badge to him and to no other proper to be given ". From Mr. O'Conor's book we learned that at the play Tailboys' references to a " bandog " annoyed the earl, because his personal badge was a greyhound. And now the earl asserts that the libel of 1590 was " published in most foul, slanderous, riming and railing sort, as it were by way of poetry ".

Here the amusing thing is that of three defendants charged by the earl, the only one who failed to appear and answer was Tailboys himself, the real culprit. William Hall, his brother-in-law, admitted that he had heard the poem "read by Mr. Talboys Dymocke the maker thereof"; and he thought that it contained matter "tending as well to the defaming of a lady in Lincolnshire as also to the dishonor of" the Earl of Lincoln.

The other defendant, Tailboys's brother, John Dymoke of Coningsby, confessed that a certain book came into his hands, "which he did read and publish at his own house in the presence and in the hearing of his wife and family". The said book, he continues, "is entitled 'Faunus his Four Poetical Furies'; and . . . is divided into four parts, *videlicet*, into an exordium showing the ground of the discourse; the second dilating upon his native soil, the antiquity of his house and the honorable tenure of the same and lastly the miserable ruin of the same; the third discanteth of the marring of his brother Satirus . . .; and the fourth the metamorphosis." John Dymoke thinks his brother Tailboys still has the book in his possession, and that he composed it "to the end to bewray his own discontentments". Finally he says that "the book doth touch the said Earl of Lincoln's son or another of that county, as by the scanning of the said book itself may appear". A passage here gives us to think: "The *marring* of his brother Satirus." The word is clearly *marring*, not *marrying*, and I conclude that in this section Tailboys enlarges on the damage his brother Sir Edward has sustained by the attacks of their malevolent uncle.

All this is highly interesting and tantalizing.   Here
we have evidence of a long poem, ' Faunus his Four
Poetical Furies ', written by Tailboys Dymoke in a
pastoral - allegorical - autobiographical - satirical   vein.
And although there is now no other trace of the
poem itself, its description gives us valuable hints of
the scope and meaning of the literary labours of the
spirited but discontented gentleman.   To add to the
vestiges of the May-games play called the ' Death of
the Lord of Kyme ', our inquiries, then, have un-
covered a long published poem, ' Caltha Poetarum ',
and traces of another, ' Faunus his Four Poetical
Furies ', all by Tailboys Dymoke.   This is an output
sufficient to give the household of Sir Edward Dymoke
a literary tinge, and to make us ask whether there is
not perhaps some link to be found between these
Dymokes and one of the greater Elizabethan poets.

A quick glance round discovers a connection of
some sort with no less a name than Samuel Daniel's.
We need not be reminded that Daniel in his own day
stood well in the first rank of poets.   Hardly had he
published his ' Sonnets to Delia ', his narrative poem
' The Complaint of Rosamond ', and his closet drama
' Cleopatra ', when Edmund Spenser saluted him in
verse :

> . . .   there is a new shepheard late upsprong
> The which doth all afore him far surpasse
> Appearing well in that well-tunéd song
> Which late he sung unto a scornfull lasse.
> Yet doth his trembling Muse but lowly flie,
> As daring not too rashly mount to hight,
> And doth her tender plumes as yet but trie
> In love's soft laies and looser thoughts delight ;
> Then rouze thy feathers quickly, *Daniell*,

And to what course thou please thy selfe advance.
But most me seemes thy accent will excell
In tragic plaints and passionate mischance.

And Francis Meres a few years later, naming the
best lyrical poets, gives " Spenser (who excelleth in
all kinds), Daniel, Drayton, Shakespeare, Breton ".
What then is known of Daniel's connection with
the Dymokes ? The references are two. The first,
Daniel's dedication of his earliest work, a translation
in 1585 of the Italian Paulus Jovius's tract on *imprese*
or devices, runs : " To the Right Worshipful Sir
Edward Dimmock, Champion to her Majestie, Samuel
Daniel wisheth happie health with increase of worship."
And he continues, " if herein I shall any way satisfie
the delight of the studious Gentlemen, you alone are
to receiue the guerdon of their fauorable voyces, whose
offered courtesie hath enforced me to undertake the
tillage of so hard a soyle, to make you a present of the
first fruits thereof."

Daniel's acknowledgment of Dymoke's " offered
courtesy " may mean no more than that the Queen's
Champion encouraged him to the work, and offered
to sponsor its publication. It has been conjectured,
however, that Daniel accompanied Sir Edward
Dymoke on an Italian journey.

The second reference comes sixteen years later. A
kinsman of Sir Edward's translated Guarini's ' Il
Pastor Fido ' before 1602, and Samuel Daniel con-
tributed to the publication a sonnet of compliment
addressed to Sir Edward Dymoke.

So much for what is known of the connection,
which is suggestive but inconclusive. Now for a
sample of the unexpected light thrown obliquely by

a search in the legal records. I find that the inevitable
Earl of Lincoln brought an action against his nephew
the Champion in the Court of Queen's Bench for
scandalum magnatum or slander of a peer. The charge
runs that at Tattershall on March 1st, 1592, Dymoke
had written a letter to Lord Lincoln's son Thomas
Lord Clinton, in part as follows :

" Now admit, though his Lordship by his perver-
sions color his murder and piracies so that for default
of evidence nothing is proceeded against him by the
common law, . . . yet if her Majesty, seeing his
indirect dealing, grievous and intolerable, did hang
him by her martial law which belongeth to her
imperial prerogative, he cannot say but it is lawful ;
and she may do it, though perhaps he would be
somewhat partial and say it were the uttermost of
law. I could bring many instances touching this
matter, and could make relation of an infinite number
of grievances offered by your father—some against
his brother, some against his kinsmen, some against
his neighbours of the better and inferior sort, some
at home, some abroad ; but because my intent is not
to make a volume of his evils but to show you an
ensample of the evil which darkens the reputation
of honour in the nobleman, I will here end, assuring
your worship I fear the many complaints against your
father to the Council, the libels daily spread against
him, the warnings of his friends, and the perils that
lately he hath escaped be but forerunners to his destruc-
tion. For of oppression comes hardness of heart, of
hardness of heart comes desperation, of desperation,
death. And surely a persuasion of mischief kindled
in men's hearts against him, as it seems it is, cannot

but burst out to his ruin. And it will happen that
he will be thought a good surgeon that setteth his
hand to the cutting away of so corrupt a member."

No question but that here is an ominous letter,
written by the champion in bitterness and hatred.
In his defence in court, Dymoke related that on
February 20th, 1592, he asked the earl his uncle for
a reconciliation of their discords, but the earl replied
only by a personal assault. He then wrote this letter,
but as his friends dissuaded him from sending it, he
gave it to his servant Samuel Daniel to be burnt.
Daniel, however, put it into a hole in the wall of
Dymoke's house in Lincoln. Four years afterwards
Dymoke sold this house to his uncle, and shortly after
the wall in which the letter was concealed was pulled
down, and the letter found amongst the stones.

What a chain of coincidence ! If Samuel Daniel
had not disobeyed orders and tucked this explosive
letter into a crack in a wall ; if Dymoke had not sold
his house to his capital enemy ; if that enemy had
not decided to pull down that particular wall, he
would never have seen the letter. But he did see it,
and brought an action in a raging temper ; the record
containing the new information about Daniel was
engrossed in routine fashion on the rolls of the Queen's
Bench, where it was left for me to find while searching
for some light on the minor poet Tailboys Dymoke.

Two definite bits of fact about Samuel Daniel
emerge from this quarrel of long ago. First, he was
in the service of Sir Edward Dymoke, and second, he
was living at Lincoln in March, 1592. Fixed points
in the early career of Daniel are not numerous, and
this small contribution may prove useful. One would

not suppose the neighbourhood of the Earl of Lincoln favourable to amorous poetry, but Daniel had published some of his ' Sonnets to Delia ' in the year preceding, and completed their publication shortly after hiding this grim letter in the wall.

With this background of new knowledge about the poetic activity of Tailboys Dymoke and his intimacy of association with the well-languaged Daniel, it is high time that we returned to our neglected ' Caltha Poetarum '. In his preface, Tailboys Dymoke mentions but four modern poets, and one of these is his friend Daniel, whom he celebrates for his versified ' History of the Civil Wars ' : '' The flower of our age, sweet pleasing *Sidney*. *Tasso* the Graue. Pollished *Daniel* the Historick. *Spencer* the Truthes Faith.''

The first qualities that strike the attention in Dymoke's work are its independence, its raciness, and its cheerful natural tone. He begins with a disarming appeal for homely country poetry : '' Gentlemen & others, I pray you let vs holde together for the preseruation of our reputation, and maintain the prescription of our lowe subiects, least *Apollos* musick do quite drowne poore *Pan*, and the countrey Hornpipe be laid aside. Alas, if the woods, the poore brooks, and the dales of the countrey, sound not sometime in our eares, as well as the Prince of *Rivers*, let the lasses give over laaking in the greene, and dauncing about the Maypole.''

Now for the allegory of the poem. It seems clear enough both from the words of G.S. and in the course of the poetry that by his figure of the Bumble Bee, Tailboys means himself ; and that by Caltha, his '' virgin Marigold '', he no doubt means one of Queen

Elizabeth's maids of honour, and by Primula, the Daisy, he means a sister of this maid of honour. But of this more later. For the moment, let us hear the poet introducing them :

> My Herball booke in Folio I vnfold,
>   I pipe of Plants, I sing of sommer flowers,
> But chiefly on the Mayden Marygold,
>   and of the Daisie, both braue Belamours :
> Trophies for Kings, Imprese for Emperours,
> Garlands to beare vpon the braue Ensignes
> Of Knights, of Peeres, of princely Palladines.
>   . . . . . .
> The next my pretie Marygold displaies,
>   her golden bloome like to the sunny beames
> Spreading abroad her rich and radyent rayes,
>   resembling *Titan* in his hottest streames,
> Euen in the glory of his Summer gleames :
> So shynes my Marygold, so doth she showe,
> So as she seemes a second Sun belowe.
>   . . . . . .
> On her attends the Dasie dearly dight,
>   that pretie Primula of Lady *Ver*,
> As hand-maid to her mistresse day and night,
>   so doth she watch, so waiteth she on her,
> With double diligence and dares not stir,
> A fairer flower perfumes not forth in May,
> Then is this Daisie, or this Primula.

The story of the poem is briefly as follows. In this garden the Bee falls in love with the Marigold ; and building a curious temple of wax, he inaugurates a new and heretical religion—Caltha-worship. Venus causes the spider to catch him in his web. This done, she presents him to her son Cupid on a leash. But he escapes, and being disdained by Caltha, he wanders abroad, visiting Italy, the country of the scorpions, and the kingdom of the Cantharides (? Spain).

Caltha, unknown to him, is now at Ephesus (London) in the court of Diana (Elizabeth). When he comes to court, the Bee at once buzzes round her. She cries, and Diana comes to catch him. The goddess turns him into a man, and, at his request, into a great musician, Musæus. In his new shape he furnishes marvellous music for the court, and teaches Diana's lovely lasses to dance.

Sister Primula is to be married at Lincoln to the loathsome Mandrake, and Caltha sends Musæus to her there with a message. Arriving, he finds Venus, who naturally does not recognize him for the Bee she had tormented, and he takes a sweet revenge on her. Caltha seems destined to marry the Woodbine Tree, who has long sued for her hand, and the Bumble Bee is left to mourn.

Such, roughly speaking, is the story. For a time I thought I had found the key to it. I assumed that the Marigold of the Poets was Bridget Manners, one of Queen Elizabeth's lovely maids of honour, the one whom Barnabe Barnes celebrates as the fairest flower in Gloriana's garland. For Bridget Manners' half-sister Elizabeth Morison (? Primula) married the hateful Earl of Lincoln (who would do very well for the part of the loathsome Mandrake); and afterwards Bridget Manners herself married Robert Tyrwhitt of Lincolnshire. This sounds an attractive theory, but I fear it has serious weaknesses. In the first place, Elizabeth Morison, when she married the Earl of Lincoln, was the widow of William Norreys, and consequently hardly to be described as a pretty primula ; and in the second place, Bridget Manners had been married five years when ' Caltha Poetarum ' appeared in 1599. I fancy the decisive clue lies in the Woodbine Tree. If someone deeply read in Elizabethan heraldry would tell me what gentleman bore the woodbine tree as his crest or badge, we might work out the correct solution.

A curious and contradictory feature of the problem is Dymoke's passage about the bee transformed into Musæus, the greatest musician in the land, who entertains the ladies at Diana's court. How can this apply to himself ? Tailboys was not remarkable for modesty, but his vanity knew some bounds. Is it possible—and I breathe the suggestion with the utmost diffidence—that this phase of the Metamorphosis refers to the great poet Samuel Daniel ? Some of the recorded words about Daniel throw a curious light on Dymoke's language in the ' Marigold '. In 1595 William Covell calls him the " court-deare verse-happy " Daniel ; and in the very year of Dymoke's publication Michael Drayton addressed Daniel as " the sweet Musæus of these times ". There is a legend that Daniel was called poet laureate after Spenser ; it is known that he had some position at court, and in 1602 Davison called him Prince of English Poets. And Tailboys Dymoke knew as well as anyone that the half-legendary Musæus was a poet rather than a musician.

I cannot profess to unravel the tangled skein of allusion, but I think you will agree with me that it is most curious and interesting. Not least impressive is the deep and particular knowledge that Tailboys Dymoke shows of the art of music, using several terms which do not appear in the ' New English Dictionary '. The scene is Diana's transformation of the Bee :

Now doth she frame her metamorphosin
  And with her blessed bookes of diuination,
She commeth to transforme and coniure him,
  And strangely workes his transmutation,*
Casting her iust count of his constellation :
And suddenly the bumble Bee as than,
Did take the shape and very forme of Man.

     . . . . .

Then madam (said he) when I was a Bee,
  I spent my dayes amongst the flowers springing,
And merie made me with my melody,
  with buzing and with huzing alwaies singing,
Whilest to my Bees, my hony I was bringing.
So that I still retaine in disposition,
And much would giue to be a good musition.

And now *Diana* doth present the man,
  with learned Lutes, & finest Virginals :
With deepe Bandoras Diapasan,
  and with the cleare well sounding Clarigals,
With subtle Sagbut, and the loud Cimbals,
And with that best beloued lulling Lyer,
With other wanton Instruments of wyer.

The Kingly Harp, for and the courtly Citheren,
  the Solace, Vyols, and the Vyolins :
The litle fidling Kit, and ancient Gittern,
  with those same faire and famous Orpherins,
With Bagpipes, Cornets, and the Cymphanins.
And now no more ycleape him bumble Buz,
But call him by the name of *Musœus*.

Now *Musœus* is maister of that Art,
  and onely rare musitian in that land :
Who cunningly can play his pricksong part,
  with ready Aroake, & nimble learned hand,
With sweet deuision of profound deskand :
His discords with true concords to agree,
Which oft is seene in Musiques subtletee.

        * *Printed* transumtation.

In Tablatury doth he take much paine,
    and by his learned line his rule and rod :
He pricks down quauers in his pleasant vaine,
    and merily he driues a minim od,
Which maketh musicke for the mightie God.
With cratchets, Semibriefs, with large & longs,
That closeth vp sweet ends in all our songs.

Long liued he amongst these louely lasses,
    and was their chief delight & onely treasure :
And taught yᵉ dames to dance their cinquepace,
    and for to foot & tread their solemn measure,
And long he sported with them at his pleasure,
Till *Caltha* she desirous on a day,
Must needs send to her sister *Primula*.

The more one grows acquainted with Tailboys
Dymoke, the more one is tempted to see in him a
kind of Mercutio in real life. Here is the same
wanton gaiety and satirical wit, combined with a
delicate English fancy of folklore and nature. What
glimpses have we from Mr. O'Conor's book of Tailboys
Dymoke in the flesh ?

Sitting on horseback outside a Tattershall tippling-
house, he is said to have called to the hostess,
" Commend me, sweetheart, to my lord of Lincoln,
and tell him that he is an ass and a fool. Is he my
uncle, and hath no more wit ? " Again, we see him
writing, producing and acting (clearly the very life
of the thing) a May-games play, in which he makes
use of local folklore—Bayard's Leap on Ancaster
Heath, and a quotation from the lost Book of Mab.

As everyone knows, in Shakespeare Queen Mab
comes alive only on the lips of Mercutio :

Mer. O ! then I see Queen Mab hath been with you.
Ben. Queen Mab ! What's she ?
Mer. She is the fairies' midwife, and she comes
In shape no bigger than an agate stone
On the forefinger of an alderman,
Drawn with a team of little atomies
Athwart men's noses as they lie asleep :
Her waggon-spokes made of long spinners' legs ;
The cover, of the wings of grasshoppers ;
The traces, of the smallest spider's web . . ."

Tailboys Dymoke's wantonness of speech, of which I am far too well-behaved to give you samples, is out of the same box as Mercutio's : gross, but gay and natural. He lives like Mercutio in an atmosphere of brawls and fights between two great and neighbouring houses. Like Mercutio again he dies early—Tailboys disappeared in the winter of 1602—but unlike Mercutio he no doubt leaves a curse on one house only, that of his pernicious uncle.

If for a moment we care to lay the reins on fancy's neck, we may imagine that Tailboys Dymoke, entered at Lincoln's Inn in the autumn of 1584, was the gayest, quickest of tongue, and most satirical of that bold young company ; that the youthful Shakespeare was fascinated by him ; and instead of Bee into Musæus, Tailboys in the poet's limbeck was metamorphosed into Mercutio.

We shall leave him with the scene he paints of the tricking of the unsuspecting Venus, who does not see that Musæus is the Bumble Bee transformed, and of the musician's sportive irony in his delicate ' Charming of the Bee ' :

Now *Venus* and the craftie fidler goes
   into a close faire arbour for to walke
Adorned with darnecks of the Damask Rose,
   whilest *Venus* enters into this same talke,
And proudly in her stateliness doth stalke :
And toong-ripe in her rhetorick doth run,
And to *Musæus* thus her tale begun.

Musæus quoth she, I must tell thee here,
   within this garden haunts a bumble Bee :
But by the way, ile bind thee for to sweare,
   not to reveale, or prate my priuitie :
But silence vse in this my secresie.
And sweares the fidler to his good abearing,
Whilest her faire sweet lips were the books of swearing.*

Fidler quoth she (so onwards on her tale)
   I have so often plagued this same Bee ;
And many times have made him ill to ayle
   As I am very fearfull of the flee,
That he will come and be reuenged on mee.
And therefore fidler watch me least I slumber,
And so the Bumble come and do me cumber.

The good Musæus answered her grace,
   and said (sweet Lady) take no thought for that,
And forthwith from his crowd or fiddle case,
   he cuts a peece of leather as he sat,
And makes a butcher's bable or flee-flap.
That if the bumble Bee come thither humming,
Musæus sweares, his bable it shall bumme him.

In meane while he is scraping on his crowd,
   onely to keepe the wanton Lady waking :
And in the Ela note he fiddles lowd,
   Whilest that she laugheth at his merry laking :
And much commends the mirth that he is making.
And from her litle finger takes a Ring,
And giues *Musæus* it, and bids him sing.

* Compare the kissing " by the book " in ' Romeo and Juliet '.

The fidler singeth like a Nightingale,
  And now his ballad and his song must bee,
Instituled, a Grandam or an old wiues tale,
  The coniuring or charming of the Flee,
And here the song ile set you downe to see :
That pretie courtly Ladyes may it keep,
To blesse them from the Bumble ere they sleep :

THE CHARMING OF THE BEE

Auant from vs false bumble Bee
  in thy busie buzing :
And come not here thou craftie Flee
  harme not in thy huzing.
Fly farre enough prodigious Fowle,
  in thy bitter stinging :
Worse then the scrytching ougly Owle,
  neuer good luck bringing.
In thy comming or thy bumming,
If thou commest hither humming
  thou false bumble Bee
In thy swarming and thy harming,
If thou chance within my charming,
      Exorciso te.

Be ware I say thou litle bird
  of my leather flee flap :
And come not here nor hitherward,
  least it reach a sound rap :
For it shall beate thy litle bum,
  Here me pretie fellow
And clap it thriftly if thou come,
  harken what I tell you.
In thy comming or thy bumming,
If thou commest hither humming
  thou false bumble Bee
In thy swarming and thy harming,
If thou chance within my charming,
      Exorciso te.

In nomine O domine
    defend vs from this Drone :
And charme this hurtfull hony Bee,
    to let us here alone.
Away thou foule and fearefull spright
    and thou little divel
I charge the come not in our sight
    for to do us evil.
  In thy comming or thy bumming,
  If thou commest hither humming
    thou false bumble Bee
  In thy swarming and thy harming,
  If thou chance within my charming,
      Exorciso te.

NOTE.—Since this paper was read, I have seen Dr. Mark Eccles's valuable contribution, " Samuel Daniel in France and Italy ", to the North Carolina *Studies in Philology*, vol. xxxiv (April, 1937), pp. 148–167. Besides establishing the probability that in 1591 Daniel was in Italy with Sir Edward Dymoke, Dr. Eccles here promised a further paper which would deal with the Lincoln—Dymoke suit of 1592, which I have treated above on pp. 57–59. We have evidently come upon this suit independently.

DIALECT IN LITERATURE.

By Sir William A. Craigie, M.A., D.Litt., LL.D.,
F.R.S.L.

[Read February 16th, 1938.]

In any language which has developed those differences of form and vocabulary which constitute a dialect or dialects, there are two periods when these may become a distinct feature in the literature of that language. In some the beginnings of literature, and even the creation of a great literature, may come after the formation of distinct dialects, each supreme within its own area, and cultivated independently without any sense of inferiority or even of rivalry. So it was in ancient Greece. The Aeolians, the Dorians, the Ionians on both sides of the Aegean, were already using very distinct varieties of Greek before Sappho, or Pindar, or Herodotus, or the Athenian dramatists began to write. The greater portion of classical Greek literature, indeed, belongs to the period before a common literary language had reduced the dialects to a position of general inferiority, although some might still be used for special purposes. Similarly in English the literature which arose in the centuries following upon the Norman Conquest, when a new language had practically to be created, was essentially a literature of dialects, in which the authors of the ' Owl and Nightingale ' or of the

' Pearl ', Chaucer, or Gower, or Lydgate, each wrote
in the form of speech which was natural to him and
his fellows, without caring how their contemporaries
in other parts of the country might express themselves. They all wrote English, as all the Hellenic
authors had written Greek, without troubling about
the obvious fact that both the forms of the words,
and even the words themselves, might be strange or
unintelligible to some of those who would in time
read their works.

In all languages where a similar situation has
existed, there comes a period when the dialects lose
this position of proud equality, when for one reason
or another they fall into obscurity, and cease to be
employed as a normal means of literary expression.
During that period, be it long or short, the dialects
survive mainly or entirely in speech, and they owe
their continued existence, and sometimes real development, to the simple fact that a great part of the
population talk more than they write, or in fact, talk
and do *not* write. The dialects are thus by no means
dead, in spite of their disappearance from literature ;
they may in fact be maintaining a very vigorous
existence within their own sphere. The importance
of this for literature is that they are immediately
available as literary material whenever the sur-
roundings in which they have been preserved become
sufficiently interesting to attract the attention of
writers or of the reading public. This usually is
the result of a change in literary tastes, a breaking-
away from a classical or conventional style, and a
return to more familiar, more homely themes. So
far as dialect thus recovers some small share in the

national literature, the recovery is due to two classes of authors, the poets and the novelists, as we shall see later on. Here, then, we have the second period when dialects become of literary importance in a language.

Although it only incidentally touches our main theme, it is interesting to note that although a tendency to break up into dialects is characteristic of most languages, there is no uniformity in the extent to which they do so, nor in the stage of their history at which it may take place. Dialects do at times correspond to natural geographical or political boundaries, but this is not always the case. It might also be supposed that languages which cover a large area would be more liable to break up into dialects than those which are concentrated within a small one, but this is far from being so. In ancient Greek a surprising number and variety of dialects were formed at an early date within the comparatively small limits of the Hellenic world. There is more variation within the few square miles covered by the North Frisian dialects of Slesvig than in the whole of Roumania or in a thousand leagues of Russia. Small isolated communities naturally tend to produce different dialects, as in the valleys of Norway or the islands of the Faeroe group, but in Iceland under similar local conditions there are practically no dialectal differences. This is commonly explained as the result of isolation and a continuous literary interest, but this explanation fails to account for a language like Lithuanian, which was never isolated and never had more than a rudimentary popular literature, showing a much smaller dialectal development

than the majority of the more recent languages of
Europe.

It is obvious that with this initial variety in the
conditions, there can be no uniformity in the extent
to which dialect appears, or has appeared, in the
various literatures. A comparative survey would
be interesting, but as no more typical example can
be found than English, it will be most natural, as
well as most practical, to limit our attention to
that.

If the Angles, Saxons, and Jutes, when they came
into England, or after they settled there, had all
been equally interested in literature, or equally
successful in cultivating it in poetry or prose, we
should have had from the Anglo-Saxon period a
literature in several independent dialects, such as
flourished in ancient Greece. Instead of this, in the
earlier period we find only the Angles, and perhaps
only the northern branch of these, active in the
production of poetry, and even this, with the exception of few fragments, has been preserved only in a
different dialect from that in which it was composed.
The outstanding feature of Anglo-Saxon literature,
as we now possess it, is that a standard form of
speech from at least the days of King Alfred succeeded
in asserting itself against the various dialects. West-
Saxon became the recognized literary form to such an
extent that our knowledge of the other dialects is
very limited, and commonly due to the accidental
preservation of a single text.

The subordination of the dialects to a standard
form of speech, which had thus taken place, and
which apparently was absolute during the eleventh

century, was destroyed by the collapse of Anglo-Saxon literature which followed upon the Conquest. Nothing shows more clearly how complete that collapse was than the absolute independence of the Middle English dialects when literature began to revive about the year 1200. Things had fallen back into practically the same condition as prevailed five or six hundred years before. If anyone chose to write in his native tongue instead of in French or Latin, he had no standard to follow except the English which he spoke himself, and which was used by those around him. By this time the original differences between the dialects had become accentuated, and minor groups had formed, or were in process of formation, within the larger. The southern dialects had been more conservative, or had developed on lines which strongly marked them off from the northern. The latter had been more progressive in the discarding of unnecessary inflexions, and in the adoption of new words from the Scandinavian settlers. The midland dialects had features in common with both—a fact which presently gave them a position of advantage, as a mean between two extremes.

Both in Old English and Middle English times, the speakers of different dialects must have been conscious of the divergences in their speech, which would sometimes render them almost unintelligible to each other. A Northumbrian and a Kentishman could not have talked with each other with any degree of ease at any period later than the tenth century. Still more must those who wrote in any dialect have been aware that they were writing an English which would be strange in any other part of the country.

Yet there is, in the earlier period, a surprising lack of reference to any difference in this respect. Even Orm, who had given serious thought to the form of his language, makes no allowance for any dialect but his own ; he merely declares without any reservation that *English* cannot be written correctly except on the lines he has laid down. (This absence of allusion to any differences, or the difficulties it might create, is, however, in accordance with the general practice in medieval literature of ignoring the difficulties of communication between those who spoke different languages.) The chief authorities on dialects must have been the scribes, who in copying texts freely altered them from other dialects to their own so completely that it is sometimes difficult to fix the original locality of a work.

It is only in the fourteenth century that we begin to find express mention of the different forms in which English was spoken in different parts of the country. Higden points out, quite correctly, that the dividing lines ran across England from east to west, so that a western man could understand an eastern man more easily than a southerner could a northerner, and consequently that a midland man was in the most advantageous position, as he could understand his neighbours both to the south and the north of him. Higden also quotes an old opinion of the northern dialect, especially as spoken in Yorkshire, which condemned it for its harshness—a verdict which his translator John of Trevisa expands with evident satisfaction. The Northerners, on the other hand, were not yet ashamed of their dialect, and speak of using " Inglis of the northern lede ", as if it were the natural thing to do. Only at a later date, about 1425, do we find a writer apologizing for possible errors in his English, on the ground that he is a northern man, and not thoroughly acquainted with the midland dialect in which he is trying to write.

As a whole, the dialects continued to flourish in literary use until about the middle of the fifteenth century. Some had given way before that time, such as Kentish and those of the southern counties. But over the greater part of England, and especially in the west and north, the local dialects still continue to be written with great purity, though after 1400 their literary importance is slight compared with that which they had in the fourteenth century. Meanwhile the speech of the capital, London, which had been strongly influenced by the East Midland dialect lying immediately to the north of it, had been steadily rising into importance, and establishing itself as a standard over a wider and wider area. Various causes co-operated in this, but especially the importance of London as a centre of commerce, law, and administration, and the wide diffusion of the writings of authors like Hoccleve and Lydgate, living in, or close to the London area. After 1450 the production of dialect literature south of the Scottish border had practically ceased, though traces of local speech naturally remain in the works of many authors. There is still room for a detailed investigation of this period, in order to bring out more clearly the stages by which dialect forms were eliminated from the literary language between 1450 and 1500.

The process which had been going on for perhaps a century was completed by the *introduction of printing.*

With such activity as Caxton, Wynkyn de Worde, and the other early printers displayed, it was inevitable that the form of the language which they adopted would establish itself as a standard. All dialects which differed in any obvious way from the language of the printers were henceforth out of the running. Over the midlands and the south of England the standard was evidently adopted with little difficulty, —the north held out a little longer, in sentiment, if not in practice. When Tyndale published the ' Examination of William Thorpe ' he modernized it for the benefit of southern readers, but at the same time had an idea of printing it in its original form for the northern men and the Scots. The north, however, made no attempt to meet the supply of southern books by the production of northern rivals. The southern standard was readily adopted by Northern writers, and before long had even forced its way into the local records of remote northern towns. So far as writing and printing were concerned, there was practically a standard English for the whole country from the beginning of the sixteenth century.

What that standard was is clearly stated by Puttenham in 1589 :

" (Our speech is) at this day the Norman English. . . .

" (A poet should employ) the most vsuall (speech) of all his countrey. . . . Our maker therfore at these dayes shall not follow Piers plowman nor Gower, nor Lydgate nor yet Chaucer, for their language is now out of vse with vs ; neither shall we take the termes of Northern-men, such as they vse in dayly talke, whether they be noble men or gentlemen, or of their best clarkes, all is a (= one) matter ; nor in effect any speach vsed beyond the riuer of Trent, though no man can deny but that theirs is the purer English Saxon at this day, yet it is not so Courtly nor so currant as our Southerne English is ; no more is the far Westerne mans speach. Ye shall therefore take the vsuall speach of the Court, and that of London and the shires lying about London within lx myles, and not much aboue. I say not this but that in euery shyre of England there be gentlemen and others that speake, but specially write, as good Southerne as we of Middlesex or Surrey do, but not the common people of euery shire, to whom the gentlemen, and also their learned clarkes, do for the most part condescend."

Writing and speech are matters of habit, and it is not necessary that the two should be in close agreement. The majority of mankind also (as I have said) speak far more than they write, and this simple fact saved the dialects of England from the extinction which appeared to threaten them. The real dialects, the actual speech of each district, still remained in regular use as the medium of every-day intercourse between man and man, although among the educated and wealthier classes it would be combined with a knowledge of the standard tongue.

Into one Anglian area, however, the standard English had not yet penetrated. Within the Scottish border the northern dialect had developed into a national tongue with a literature of its own, which between 1375 and 1500 had assumed very respectable proportions. During that period, in spite of the intense national feeling which distinguished the Scots, they continued from force of habit to call their language English. Even the fervently patriotic author of the ' Wallace ' says of the French knight Thomas de Longueville that he might have been taken for a Scot, " save for his tongue, for English had he

nane ". The political independence of Scotland,
however, and the very strong spirit of antagonism
to all that was English, gave its language an advantage
over that of the north of England, and preserved it
from the encroachments of the southern standard for
another century. The decline in the literary position
of the Scottish tongue began with the Reformation
and ended with the Union of the Crowns. The
Scottish reformers had been much in contact with
their English brethren, the English version of the
Bible lay ready to their hands, and the really patriotic
party in Scotland, the adherents of the Roman
Catholic church, were fighting in a losing cause.
There was much truth in the taunt which one of
them levelled at John Knox, declaring that he would
write to him in Latin " because I am not acquainted
with your Southern ". In Scotland, however, as in
England, the spoken dialect survived in full vigour
the disuse of it in writing.

With this important exception the English dialects
figure in the literature of the sixteenth century only
in two respects: (1) Authors continue to use words
which had only a local currency, and it is frequently
possible to identify the district to which an author
belonged by certain elements in his vocabulary. It
would, for example, be quite clear from his use of
certain words that Golding, the translator of Ovid's
' Metamorphoses', was an East Anglian, even if
there were no other evidence to prove it. Similarly,
Thomas Hudson, the translator of Du Bartas's
' Judith ', can by the same test be unavoidably convicted of being a Scot. The natural reason for this is
given in a simple, and rather touching, manner by

the Scottish poet Alexander Craig in the preface to
his 'Amorose Songes, Sonets, and Elegies ' of 1606 :

" Smyrnaean Maeonides vsed in his delicate Poems diuers
Dialects, as Ionic, Aeolic, Attic, and Doric : so haue I (O
courteous Reader) in this . . . imitate that renowned Hellenist
Homer, in vsing the Scotish and English Dialectes : the one
as innated, I can not forget ; the other as a stranger, I can
not vpon the sodaine acquire."

(2) The dramatists, and occasionally other writers,
used a conventional south-western dialect as the
proper speech for unlettered rustics, regardless of
the locality in which the scene was laid. Examples
of this are familiar from Shakespeare, as when
Edgar in King Lear assumes the person and speech
of a peasant, and says, "Chill not let go, zir, without
vurther 'casion ", and, " An chud ha bin zwaggered
out of my life, 'twould not ha' bin zo long as 'tis by a
vortnight ". The intention in such cases is usually
to produce a comic effect, the dialect being accompanied by a rustic ignorance or simplicity, though
at times there is also a shrewd mother-wit, a basis of
native common sense, in the utterances of the
innocent clown.

More rarely, other dialects are represented in the
literature of the sixteenth century. In William
Bulleyn's dialogue of the ' Fever Pestilence ', of
1564, one of the speakers is a beggar who declares
that he " was borne in Redesdale in Northumberland,
and came of a wight ridyng sirname called Robsons,
good honest men and true, savyng a little shiftyng for
their living, . . . God and our Leddie help them, sillie
pure men ". The beadle of the beggars, he explains,

was also "a Redesdale man borne, a gudman and a true, which for ill will in his youth did fleem the countrie ; it was laid to his charge the driving of kine hem to his father's byre ". There is no evidence that Bulleyn himself was a Northumbrian, but so far as they go, the words he puts into the mouth of the beggar have the true northern stamp. His speech, however, becomes less and less dialectal as the dialogue proceeds, and in the end differs little from Standard English. Bulleyn evidently became tired of writing Northumbrian, or thought that a very little of it would go a long way with his readers.

In 'Albion's England ' Warner brings in " a simple Northerne man " to declaim against monks and friars in a dozen stanzas of dialect, which is obviously artificial. There are also northern words in Spenser's ' Shepherd's Calendar ' of 1579, the dialect of which is in the main midland and southern.

Altogether, although the use of dialect by the authors of the sixteenth century is rare and incidental, there is enough of it to repay closer study than it has yet received. A complete survey of it, separating as far as possible the genuine from the artificial, would help to fill the gap which lies between the older natural use of dialect, and the conscious adoption of it as a literary medium in the period which follows.

This new interest in dialect arose out of the historical and antiquarian studies which marked the early years of the seventeenth century, and enables us to ascertain, though imperfectly, the changes which they had undergone during the period of their obscurity. About 1630, for example, we learn something about the dialect of Berkeley in Gloucestershire,

presenting features which are startling in their antiquity. The modern history of the dialects, however,
mainly dates from the last quarter of that century—
from Ray's collection of dialect words published in
1674, the printing of some Yorkshire verses a few
years later, and the beginnings of a new Scottish
vernacular poetry about the same time. Shortly
after 1700 the strongly-marked dialects of Somerset
and Lancashire induced local authors to make use of
them for humorous literature, Scottish poetry began to
attract attention, and by the middle of the century
the dialects had again taken a definite place in
literature in two respects. One of these was a
continuation, or rather a renewal, of the older practice
of introducing speakers of dialect among the other
characters of a novel, a tale, or a play, at first with
no higher purpose than that of humorous contrast,
but latterly with a deeper appreciation of the sterling
qualities of many of those who naturally used this
type of speech. The other and new feature was the
independent use of the dialects themselves in both
verse and prose in the endeavour to create a distinct
dialect literature—to give to a local form of speech
the standing of a literary language, such as it had not
possessed for several generations. This was attempted
with varying success in different parts of the country,
and had become common by the close of the eighteenth
century. Since that time it has increased in quantity,
and improved in quality, in a most remarkable
manner. We have, in fact, the curious phenomenon
that at a time when the natural living use of the
dialects is more restricted than it was, the employment
of them as a literary medium is more common, and

on a higher plane, than has been the case at any time
since the fourteenth century.

At the outset the novelists of the eighteenth century
are somewhat chary in the use of dialect, perhaps
doubtful whether it would be much appreciated by
their readers. In Smollett's ' Roderick Random ' of
1748, for example, there is less dialect than the
speakers might naturally have been expected to
use. Even Strap usually talks ordinary English. A
northern speaker, however, is made to say (c. xi) :
" Waunds, coptain, whay woan't you sooffer the poor
waggoner to meake a penny. Coom, coom, young
man, get oop, get oop, never moind the coptain ",
etc. In Fielding's ' Tom Jones ' of the same date the
dialect which occurs in the earlier chapters is south-
western, and is used at times even by Squire Alworthy.
Samples of it are : " I don't know, measter, *un't*
I. An't please your honour, here *hath* been a *vight* ",
and " It will do'*n* no harm with *he* "—the latter a
genuine piece of south-western grammar. Twenty
years later Smollett in ' Humphrey Clinker ' (1771)
introduces both Cockneyisms, as " upon the ving ",
" with a vitness ", " a varrant ", " vax candles "
" a fellor ", etc., and Scottish dialect, as " I wadna
be guilty o' sic presumption for the wide warld ", and
" By my saul, I'se neer trouble Providence again ".
Smollett's interest in dialect, however, is most clearly
shown in the same work in his account of the argu-
ments by which Lieutenant Lismahago maintained
the superiority of the Scottish manner of speech to
that of England.

It is only with the work of Sir Walter Scott and
his contemporaries that dialect in fiction becomes

more than a mere incidental touch, adding some local colour to the narrative, and becomes an integral part of the story or novel, without which it would lose the greater part of its charm, or indeed have no reason for being written at all. Such tales as ' Guy Mannering ', ' The Antiquary ', ' Old Mortality ' or ' Rob Roy ' could no doubt have been told without the use of dialect, but only with the loss of some of their finest features, and the same thing holds of a large number of novels written during the past century. It is not merely that dialect plays a larger part in these than it did in the eighteenth century ; it is used with a different purpose and on a different plane. It not only becomes an essential part of the story ; it is used seriously and serves to bring out thoughts and feelings as deep and as touching as any that can be expressed in standard English. It is in this form, indeed, that dialect makes its widest appeal, being readily read and appreciated by thousands of readers who would remain indifferent to anything, however excellent, that was written entirely in dialect.

It is not every writer, of course, who can use dialect in this way both successfully and correctly. The success of any literary form is apt to produce imitators, and authors are thus tempted to introduce dialect speakers among their characters without any real knowledge of the speech they would naturally use, and often ignorant of the fact that dialects are even less tolerant of variations from their norm than the standard language is. The dialect in such a novel as Lytton's ' Paul Clifford ', for instance, is an example of this. Fortunately for writers of this class, most of their readers are equally ignorant, and are willing to accept as genuine dialect anything which varies from the usual form of English. It is only the native of the particular district who will readily discover the fraud, and be either scornful or resentful according to his nature or his mood.

The independent use of dialect as a literary medium developed more rapidly and more successfully than its employment as a feature in fiction. There is certainly no great literary merit in the ' Yorkshire Dialogues' in verse of 1673 and 1684, however interesting and valuable they may be to the student of dialect, nor can any higher place be claimed for the ' Exmoor Courtship' and ' Scolding' of 1746 and 1747, or the Lancashire works of John Collier, writing under the name of Tim Bobbin, beginning at the same date. Indeed, although the total amount of English dialect writing between 1700 and 1800 is considerable, there is no page in it that would naturally appear in any anthology of English verse or prose for that century. The other side of the Border had been far more successful, possibly because the Scottish literary tradition had never been entirely broken. The new way which had been shown by the Semples of Beltrees, and others of lesser note, was raised by Allan Ramsay to a level which attracted attention outside of Scotland, his collected works being published at London in 1731 and at Dublin in 1733. In particular, his ' Gentle Shepherd' of 1725 attracted so much attention as a pastoral play, fitting in with the taste of the times, that it imme- diately gave a secure place to the use of the Scottish dialect in poetry. His immediate successor, and in some respects a better poet, Robert Fergusson, never attracted the same attention, but was the necessary link between Ramsay and Burns, in whom modern Scottish poetry attained its highest level, and henceforward claimed no mean place in the annals of English literature.

After 1800 both England and Scotland show a surprising increase in the volume of dialect verse and prose which they produce. This is by no means equally distributed, Scotland and the northern counties having a far greater productivity than the midlands or the south. The quality also varies very greatly in the different areas, a very large proportion of the whole being of more value as specimens of dialect than of literature. The test of this is the limited extent to which dialect authors figure in the ordinary histories of English literature or in any of the numerous anthologies.

It does not follow from this that dialect literature in itself is necessarily of an inferior stamp. Its comparative failure in competition with what is written in standard English is due to a variety of causes which only a genius like that of Burns can successfully overcome. The defect lies partly in the writers themselves, partly in the subjects with which they most naturally deal—subjects of limited interest in the treatment of which the use of the dialect vocabulary is appropriate. If really of a high order, the value of such writing is largely sentimental ; it makes a very simple, though very direct, appeal to the feelings of those to whom the language is familiar. It trusts for its effect to familiar associations of an intimate, and often trivial nature. It touches the

heart, or tickles the fancy, because it speaks of
homely things in a homely manner, and in this way
obtains attention and appreciation from many who
have no interest in literature for its own sake.   To the
outsider, a large proportion of dialect literature seems
trivial and even vulgar, and judged by purely literary
or aesthetic standards it undoubtedly is so.   But the
outsider can never understand the effect which it
will have on those to whom the particular dialect is a
natural form of expression, and to whom its words and
phrases are full of meaning derived from early associations.   It is for this reason that the art of writing
in dialect, when it has once obtained a vogue, may
still appeal to a large body of readers, and may easily
outlast the general use of dialect in ordinary life.

While this direct appeal to the feelings gives dialect
literature its chief strength, and indeed is one of the
main reasons for its existence, it also constitutes one
of its weaknesses.   Outside of a certain audience the
appeal loses much of its effect, or may fail altogether.
When I read a book, say of humorous sketches, written
in my own Scottish dialect, I can appreciate every
point which the author has tried to make, because
not only the meaning, but all the associations of each
word and phrase are familiar to me.   But when I
turn to a work of exactly the same type in a Lancashire
or Yorkshire dialect, I feel that although the same
merits are clearly there, it is impossible for me to
appreciate them in the same way.   The sentences
which would move the native of Bradford or Leeds
to laughter or tears will leave me quite unmoved;
for me they have no breath of life, simply because
the turns of expression which they employ so aptly

have not formed part of my daily experience. Even the commonest phrases may acquire a deep significance from this cause, when both author and reader thoroughly understand each other. So subtle indeed are the associations of a dialect that it is usually impossible to alter a single word in a song or saying, or even a phrase, without destroying its character and making it ridiculous. The poetry of one language may be successfully reproduced in another by a skilled translator ; to transpose dialect poetry into the standard language is an impossibility.

Another serious disadvantage under which the literature of any dialect labours is not readily appreciated except by those who speak it. To the reader who is familiar only with standard English the oral element of a dialect matters little ; he judges it, or appreciates it, merely by the appearance it makes on the printed page, without realizing that this gives him only a part of the truth. He may even be so far unconscious of this as to believe that he can read aloud a dialect passage with a fair approximation to the real sounds. This is a delusion which can only be held by those who have never spoken, or never been accustomed to hear, genuine dialect. Every dialect, even every subdivision of a dialect, has its peculiarities, not only in its broader features, but in its subtle nuances, which no outsider can hope to reproduce successfully. The speaker of good English may suffer when he hears it spoken badly or incorrectly, but his feelings are likely to be mild compared to one who hears his own dialect mangled by tongues unaccustomed to utter it. The more intimately a speaker is acquainted with one dialect, the more he realizes the futility of attempting to imitate any other. I once illustrated this at New-castle by reading some verses in Northumbrian dialect with my own Scottish pronunciation, much to the amusement of the audience, and then having them read by a real Northumbrian. Even within such areas as Scotland or Yorkshire, or even smaller portions of the country, one cannot with impunity trespass on adjacent and closely related dialects. I can, for example, read with perfect confidence anything written in the central Scottish dialect, where the local variations are not obtrusive, and I think I may justifiably illustrate my point by doing so, even at the risk of being barely understood. Robert Fergusson's poem of ' The Farmer's Ingle ' (which clearly suggested ' The Cottar's Saturday Night ' of Burns) begins with this verse :

" Whan gloamin' grey out owre the welkin keeks ;
    Whan Bawtie ca's his owsen to the byre ;
  Whan thrasher John, sair dung, his barn-door steeks,
    An' lusty lasses at the dightin' tire ;
  What bangs fu' leal the e'ening's comin' cauld,
    An' gars snaw-tappit Winter freeze in vain ;
  Gars dowie mortals look baith blithe an' bauld,
    Nor fley'd wi' a' the poortith o' the plain ;
    Begin, my Muse, and chant in hamely strain."

Further on he describes the children listening to their grandmother's tales in these words :

" In rangles round afore the ingle's lowe,
    Frae gude-dame's mouth auld-warld tales they hear,
  O' warlocks loupin' round the wirrikow,
    O' ghaists that win in glen and kirkyaird drear,
    Which touzles a' their tap, and gars them shake wi' fear.

" For weel she trows that fiends and fairies be
    Sent frae the de'il to fleetch us to our ill ;
That kye ha'e tint their milk wi' evil e'e,
    And corn been scowdered on the glowin' kiln.
Oh, mockna this, my friends, but rather murn,
    Ye in life's brawest spring wi' reason clear ;
Wi' eild our idle fancies a' return,
    And dim our dulefu' days wi' bairnly fear ;
    The mind's aye cradled whan the grave is near."

Except for a few literary touches, this is genuine
dialect, as pronounced by those to whom it is the
earliest and most natural form of speech. Similarly,
if I pick up Scott's 'Antiquary ', and open it at the
page where Edie Ochiltree unkindly exposes the
delusion of Monkbarns regarding his Roman camp,
every word of the old man's speech comes readily and
exactly from my tongue :

" Ou, I ken this about it, Monkbarns, an' what profit
hae I for tellin' ye a lee ? I just ken this about it, that about
twenty years syne, I, an' a wheen hallenshakers like mysell',
and the mason-lads that built the lang dyke that gaes down
the loanin', and twa or three herds maybe, just set to wark,
and built this bit thing here that ye ca' the—the—Praetorian,
an' a' just for a bield at auld Aiken Drum's bridal, an' a bit
blithe gae-down we had in't, some sair rainy weather. Mair
by token, Monkbarns, if ye howk up the bouroch, as ye seem
to ha'e begun, ye'll find, if ye hae na fund it already, a stane
that ane o' the mason-callants cut a ladle on to ha'e a bourd
at the bridegroom, an' he put four letters on't, that's
A. D. L. L.—Aiken Drum's Lang Ladle—for Aiken was ane
o' the kale-suppers o' Fife."

Now if instead of the 'Antiquary ' I take up ' Rob
Roy ', I can read the speeches of Andrew Fairservice

or Baillie Nicol Jarvie with equal readiness, but do
you suppose that any native of Glasgow would be
satisfied with my manner of doing it ?   And if I
ever read aloud any of the dialect passages in that
masterpiece of Scottish farm-life, ' Johnny Gibb of
Gushetneuk ', it would certainly not be to an
audience of Aberdonians.   Still less should I attempt
to read ' Tim Bobbin ' to anyone from Lancashire,
or the poetry of William Barnes to a native of
Dorset.

So far as their place in literature is concerned, it
is thus an advantage to the dialects that they are so
largely taken on trust, and that errors or inaccuracies
in writing them can be detected only by a few, while
the actual sounds are a matter of no importance to
the majority of readers.   Success in using dialect for
literary ends depends more upon the interest of the
matter than on correctness in the form.

In one respect the dialects are at a great disadvantage as competitors for literary distinction.   Their
vocabulary may be copious in some respects, on
certain lines presenting even greater variety and
vigour of expression than the standard language ;
but the range, both of words and phrases, is more
limited, and usually confined to the things of every-
day life.   The writer in dialect must either limit
himself to subjects which are compatible with a
natural unconstrained use of the dialect, or, if he
attempts to transcend this, must lay himself open to
the charge of artificiality.   The actual cultivation of
a dialect for higher literary ends is certainly possible,
but the process must be slow, and in the beginning is
likely to evoke more criticism than sympathy.   Recent

interest in dialect, however, has already had a remarkable effect in some areas, such as Yorkshire, in stimulating the production of a new dialect literature, especially in poetry, with a higher tone and a greater variety of interest than had hitherto been known.

The outstanding successes of pure dialect literature are not numerous, and even of these only a few have been able to vindicate for themselves a place in English literature as a whole. Yet a survey of that literature from 1800 to the present day will show that in certain types of writing the use of dialect has frequently been a factor in success, and that not only in this country ; witness the place of Lowell's ' Biglow Papers ' in American literature. Whatever the future of the dialects may be—and on that head there is room for differences of opinion—a number of them have already established their claim to literary rank in one or other respect, and it is quite certain that some have still a career before them, possibly more distinguished than that which they have hitherto had.

THE DOWSON LEGEND.

By John Gawsworth, F.R.S.L.

[Read March 9th, 1938.]

I.

It has been Ernest Dowson's ill-fortune to have his
memory perpetuated in the writings of his slightest
acquaintances to a greater degree than in those of his
intimate friends. He, who scorned pity, has been
pitied ; he, who would have desired no explanation,
has been explained. His acquaintances have paved
a road to perdition for his character with the best
intentions and in the most glib phrases ; and, being
first in the field, have by now established a legend
that his own words, or the testimony of those closest
to him, will not easily dispel. Until the appearance
of his ' Collected Letters ', in an unexpurgated form,
we can neither hope for his deliverance, nor for a true
portrait. The reticence of his friends has already had
unfortunate results. Their discretion has strength-
ened the case of his commentators, whose hints,
hitherto unrefuted by the production of any unbowd-
lerized documentary evidence, have been avidly seized
upon, distorted, and published. Nor have those who
have taken it upon themselves to write about him
been above deluding themselves and weaving fantasies.
The information intended to damn, they have imparted,
in general, together with the most tender expressions
of compassionate regard.

Before we permit Dowson to speak for himself out of a series of twelve newly-discovered and unpublished personal letters, let us examine his legend from the day in 1900 when Mr. Arthur Symons unhappily inaugurated it in an obituary notice, afterwards included as a Preface to the first collected edition of the ' Poems ' 1905, and frequently reprinted since.

This essay, certainly the most widely-read account of the poet, has been the source of nearly every stream of calumny concerning him which has flowed in ever-widening ripples during this century.

Few will deny that the literary criticism and generous appreciation of the poetry that it contains is of that satisfying order of excellence which Dowson, were he living, would surely have wished set forth. But the fact that Mr. Symons did not know the poet sufficiently well has led him into performing the greatest disservice to Dowson's personal reputation. Indeed, Mr. Edgar Jepson, a close friend and colla-borator of the subject, has recently described the memoir as " a posthumous misfortune which may cast a perpetual slur on his name ".

To be fair to Mr. Symons, we must quote the phrases to which Dowson's family and intimate friends not unnaturally took exception, their protest being based on the grounds of inaccuracy and exag-geration.   For these phrases, as I will shortly attempt to illustrate by quotation, have been seeping in and colouring unconsciously, and in some cases less unconsciously, the imaginations and memories of writers upon Dowson for more than thirty years.

These phrases I will tabulate.   There are three sets of sentences.

One : Dowson's appearance :—

". . . A sort of Keats-like face, the face of a
demoralised Keats   . . . an appearance generally
somewhat dilapidated."

Two : " The real man " :—

". . . He was always at his best in a cabmen's
shelter. Without a certain sordidness in his surround-
ings he was never quite comfortable, never quite
himself ; and at those places you are obliged to drink
nothing stronger than coffee or tea. I liked to see him
occasionally, for a change, drinking nothing stronger
than coffee or tea. At Oxford, I believe, his favourite
form of intoxication had been haschisch. . . ."

Three : Escape from life :—

" It was only when his life seemed to have been
irretrievably ruined that Dowson quite deliberately
abandoned himself to that craving for drink, which
was doubtless lying in wait for him in his blood, as
consumption was also ; it was only latterly, when he
had no longer any interest in life, that he really wished
to die. But I have never known him when he could
resist either the desire or the consequences of drink.
. . . Under the influence of drink, he became almost
literally insane, certainly quite irresponsible. He fell
into furious and unreasoning passions ; a vocabulary
unknown to him at other times sprang up like a whirl-
wind ; he seemed always about to commit some act of
absurd violence. . . Indeed, that curious love of the
sordid, so common an affectation of the modern decadent, and with him so genuine, grew upon him, and
dragged him into more and more sorry corners of a life
which was never exactly ' gay ' to him. . . he lived
in a mouldering house, in that squalid part of the East
End which he came to know so well, and to feel so

strangely at home in. He drank the poisonous liquors of those pot-houses which swarm about the docks. . . . In Paris, Les Halles took the place of the docks. At Dieppe . . . he discovered strange, squalid haunts about the harbour. . . . At Brussels . . . he flung himself into all that riotous Flemish life, with a zest for what was most sordidly riotous in it. It was his own way of escape from life."

Thus Mr. Symons. And every copy of Dowson's 'Poems' in circulation from 1905 until the enlarged edition of 1934 contained those sentences, spread that gospel.

Naturally, it was not long before notice was taken. Having read Mr. Symons' essay, Mr. Talcott Williams, an American critic, summed Dowson up for his continent in one paragraph*: "Born in 1867, he died in 1900, having thrown away his life in such reckless and foolish dissipation as comes to few—Dowson had the best of life before him, and he chose the worst. Nor is there aught which furnishes excuse for this in the brief life prefaced by Arthur Symons."

Mr. Edgar Jepson, properly taking exception to this, protested against it, and its source, in *The Academy* of November 2nd, 1907, in an article, " The Real Ernest Dowson ", declaring that his friend had not, in fact, been " a rather disagreeable wastrel ". This refutation he accompanied with corrections of not a few of Mr. Symons' statements, and an additional page of first-hand reminiscence, for he could claim that during two years Dowson and he had spent " on the average four evenings a week together ". In 1933, after much injurious matter in literary and

---

* In *The Book News Monthly.*

journalistic memoirs had appeared, Mr. Jepson, in his ' Memories of a Victorian ', returned once more to his criticism of Mr. Symons' phrases, and this time dealt with them more fully : " When," he writes in this volume, " Mr. Symons states that Dowson felt strangely at home in that squalid part of the East End, Stepney, drinking ' the poisonous liquors of those pot-houses which swarm about the docks ', he is writing nonsense. Dowson always made the greatest possible haste, a daily haste, to get out of the East End to the society of his kind. . . . No less nonsensical is Mr. Symons' statement that Dowson loved the sordid. . . . In his hour of prosperity . . . Dowson wore a frock-coat from Savile Row and a masterpiece of Mr. Henry Heath, and more beautifully dressed than any other poet I have known, was fit to walk Bond Street. . . . With regard to his drinking, on which Mr. Symons lays such stress, during the years we perused London together Dowson would get drunk now and then. But who did not ? Nevertheless for weeks together he would be sober enough."

Although Mr. Jepson made these statements in 1907, he was forced to repeat them in 1933, for the world, in the interval, would have its way and believe what it wanted to believe. With every year more and more critics employed themselves in the service of the " romantic legend ". Mr. R. H. Sherard, in whose hospitable house Dowson died, had published an account of the poet's last hours in *The Author* of May, 1900, and provided further memories in his ' Twenty Years in Paris ', 1905. Mr. Morley Roberts also bore witness, and in America Mr. T. B. Mosher

added a new thought (one that still persists) : " It
may have been that the real Cynara was ' the daughter
of a refugee . . . reduced to keeping a humble
restaurant in a foreign quarter of London '."

Mr. Symons, referring to Dowson's unfruitful and
unrequited love for Adelaide Foltinowicz, of the
" Poland " Restaurant, 19, Sherwood Street, simply
and truthfully had never suggested that *she* was
Cynara.

The Cynara poem was collected into ' Verses ',
1896, a book dedicated to Adelaide with such declara-
tions as " To you, who are my verses. . . . This
and all my work is made for you in the first place " ;
therefore, it was concluded that she must also be the
subject of the Cynara poem. But Adelaide, in
February 1891, when ' Cynara ' was written, was
only twelve years old, and not known at that period
of her acquaintance with Dowson to be yet passion-
ately adored. Why, then, should one so unawakened
be Dowson's symbol of unique Woman ? A later
writer, Miss Marion Plarr, in her novel ' Cynara ',
1933, is plausible when she says that Dowson at this
time was " anxious to write a really good sin poem ",
but far less so when, accepting Mr. Mosher's suggestion,
she continues, "And Cynara was Innocence and
Innocence was Adelaide ". As a schoolmaster friend
of Dowson's, who often dined with him in " Poland "
in those days, put his reaction when he read this
argument of Miss Plarr's : "The incongruity of it ! One
has merely to glance at the poem to ask oneself what a
child of twelve, whom the poet had known for hardly
more than a year, could possibly be doing *dans cette
galère*."

Mr. Mosher, with his suggestion of Adelaide being Cynara, it is clear, started a hare quite as agile as those loosed by Mr. Symons. Even Mr. Jepson, in his 1933 autobiography, went chasing after it—wrongly, as he admitted to me.*

And then there were others ! One such was Guy Thorne who, in *T.P.s' Weekly* of July 11th, 1913, recalled seeing the poet " towards the end of his short and tragic life. . . . Pale, emaciated, in clothes that were almost ragged ".

Month by month, year by year, the rumours that were slowly crushing the memory of Dowson, the man, gathered strength.

II.

There was, however, at hand one other old friend, if an over-reticent one. This was the poet Victor Plarr (Miss Marion Plarr's father), whom, in 1914, we find referring to the legend as having " now grown half diabolic ", and declaring : " We, who are on the side of the Angels, refuse to give him up to the Demon, and shall die, some of us, still contesting the Dowson myth."

Plarr's act of defence was to publish a volume of Reminiscences, Unpublished Letters and Marginalia concerning Dowson's life between 1888 and 1897, something of a pioneer work, but so marred by the expurgation of personal facts from the letters that its value was half nullified. Evasions and omissions become admissions in deprecating eyes. And though Plarr stated as emphatically as Mr. Jepson that

* Mr. Jepson, who heard this paper read, and was in full agreement with the views I expressed, died on April 11th, 1938.

Dowson was no foul-mouthed inebriate (that miscon-
struction of his character being " generated chiefly in
the closely allied consciences of America and of British
Nonconformity "), and emphasized, to the point of
redundancy, that the poet's acts were " far, very far,
from the depths of lurid dissipation that is being
allowed to cover his good fame, unless it be rescued
betimes ", his assertions alone were hardly sufficient
to turn the balance of opinion. Falsification and
vilification continued unchecked, indeed, rather stimu-
lated than otherwise by the appearance of this book
intended to serve and save.

Frank Harris, in *Pearson's Magazine* for March,
1917, gossiped in an article entitled " The Swan-Song
of Youth: Ernest Dowson ", as only Frank Harris
could gossip. So that in the course of his memories it
is scarcely surprising that all Mr. Symons' recollections
reappeared as first-hand impressions, and in the
most quaint embroideries: the Keats-like face,
the dilapidation, the poisonous East End liquor, the
objectionable language, and the home-sickness for
squalor.

Mr. Louis Untermeyer, in 1920, writing of Dowson
in his American anthology of ' Modern British Poetry',
appears, also, to have been influenced by Mr. Symons'
essay, for he made the following assertions : " For
almost two years he [Dowson] lived in sordid supper-
houses known as ' cabmen's shelters '. He literally
drank himself to death."

In the same year, 1920, in England, Mr. Bernard
Muddiman, in his ' The Men of the Nineties ', stated
that Dowson " wrote of the purlieus round the docks ".
This was just incorrect. Mr. Muddiman, obliging the

legend, added more-damaging references : Dowson
" used to drink hashish and make love in Soho in the
French manner of Henri Murger's Latin Quarter" was
one; and "Ernest Dowson's indulgence in the squalid
debaucheries of the Brussels kermesse " another.

Mr. W. B. Yeats, in his 'The Trembling of the Veil"
two years later, alas appears no more chivalrous. But
it is chiefly rumour that he records.

Describing meetings at the Rhymers' Club, Mr.
Yeats admitted : " None knew as yet that Dowson,
who seemed to drink so little and had so much dignity
and reserve, was breaking his heart for the daughter
of the keeper of an Italian " (sic) " eating-house, in
dissipation and drink, and that he might that very
night sleep upon a sixpenny bed in a doss-house."
And again : Dowson was " full of sexual desire. Sober
he would look at no other woman ", [than Adelaide
Foltinowicz] " it was said, but, drunk, would desire
whatever woman chance brought, clean or dirty."

Mr. Yeats does not stop at this. Proceeding
further, he recalls that Dowson was seen drinking an
apéritif with a fille de joie in Dieppe ; that to inculcate
" a more wholesome taste " in Oscar Wilde he pro-
pelled him through the door of a brothel there ; that
he attacked a baker in Pont Aven; and adds, "The
last time I saw Dowson he was pouring out a glass of
whiskey for himself in an empty corner of my room
and murmuring over and over in what seemed
automatic apology ' The first to-day '."

In The Listener of October 14th, 1936, Mr. Yeats,
referring further to his fellow member of the Rhymers'
Club, and to the comparatively short period that he
knew him, makes two admissions, both of which can

scarcely be true : " I envied Dowson his dissipated
life." " Years were to pass before I discovered that
Dowson's life, except when he came to the Rhymers',
or called upon some friend selected for an extreme
respectability, was a sordid round of drink and cheap
harlots."

Mr. Yeats, relying on report for his crudest effects,
however, is preferable to Mrs. Gertrude Atherton,
whose vials of pity and consideration are tipped over
in an article in *Cassell's Weekly* for March 21st, 1923,
and poured forth to the lees in her 'Adventures of a
Novelist ', 1932. She, and Mr. H. A. Vachell, it
appears, met Dowson at Pont Aven, where Mr. Vachell
recognized him as " a child of the mud " and Mrs.
Atherton as " a sad-looking object shambling ", " a
trapped wild thing ", " a lost soul " suffering from
nostalgie de la boue. But the seven-and-a-half pages
dealing with her efforts to reclaim him, with her
" blood up ", her calculated flattery of him, and her
general patronage, are such monstrous reading that
I cannot bring myself to remark upon them, beyond
adding that the anecdote of the poet's assault upon
the baker is given in them again from hearsay.

Mrs. Atherton's compatriot, the eminent bookman,
John Quinn, in his biographical note on Dowson in
' The Catalogue of the Quinn Library, 1923 ', writes
sanely and honestly. He has borrowed no exaggerations from Mr. Symons, and but one fallacy : " The
East End of London, swarming, squalid, vivid,
attracted him."

Osbert Burdett, in his ' The Beardsley Period ',
1925, on the other hand, shows a mind thoroughly
attuned to Mr. Symons' conception of the position,

and writes : " Dowson's life, even in Mr. Victor Plarr's
discreet remembrance, and with Mr. Symons' warning
in mind, was a true complement of these poems, which
reflect his less oblivious moods, if with faint echoes
yet with rare fidelity."

Mr. Richard le Gallienne is equally of the set, and
Symons, tune of mind. In his 'The Romantic
Nineties ', 1926, he remembers that Dowson " was a
frail appealing figure with an almost painfully sensitive
face, delicate as a silver-point, recalling at once
Shelley and Keats, too worn for one so young, haggard,
one could not but surmise, with excessive ardours of
too eager living ".

The late nineteen-twenties, which we now reach, were
a period of comparative lull for the myth, marked by
repetitions merely.

Mr. John Lockett, in *T.P.'s Weekly* for February
25th, 1928, referred to hashish and East-End pot-
houses.

The *Sunday Express* of May 27th of the same year,
echoing Mr. Mosher, stated, "And Dowson worshipped
her [Adelaide] . . . and she is the Cynara of the
splendid poem."

Mr. Francis Gribble, in his volume of personal
reminiscences, ' Seen in Passing ', 1929, recalled
strong language, absinthe, and that "hashish, they
say, was Dowson's most formidable enemy ".

It would seem that invention in these years was at
a low ebb.

III.

We come to the last phase of the legend—its
progress during the present decade

Mr. Ernest Rhys, in his entertaining ' Everyman Remembers ', 1931, uninfluenced by his reading, adds nothing to the myth, but writes of Dowson scrupulously and with respect and regard. Sir William Rothenstein, in his first volume of ' Men and Memories ', published the same year, is less happy ; Mr. Symons had stated in one place that Dowson deliberately abandoned himself to his craving for drink ; and, in another, that he really wished to die. With Sir William these suggestions re-emerged in new shape—combined : *i. e.* Dowson, desiring to die, destroyed himself deliberately.

Here is the short passage : " Poor Dowson was a tragic figure. While we others amused ourselves, playing with fireworks, Dowson meant deliberately to hurt himself. While for Beardsley, perversities were largely an attitude he adopted *pour épater les bourgeois.* I doubt if Dowson wanted to live ; he was consumed by a weary hopelessness, and he drank, I thought, to be rid of an aspect of life too forlorn to be faced."

Nor is this all that Sir William has to tell of the " homeless, miserable, and unkempt " poet.

He enhances the decadent atmosphere of his memory by recalling an anecdote of the eternal cabmen's shelters and confessing : " It was not always easy to get him away when he was very drunk, nor past some poor street walker, who would seize his arm, and try to inveigle him to her lodging."

In 1932 Dowson's drunkenness was again the object of comment in a volume of reminiscences, this time in Mr. Grant Richards' ' Memories of a Misspent Youth '.

In *John o' London's Weekly* for September 30th,
1933, Mr. Morley Roberts (unabashed by Victor
Plarr's 1914 description of him as writing " from
hearsay ", a " brilliant weaver of fancies "), repeated
his earlier astonishing delineation of a symposium
which began with Dowson, Lionel Johnson and Plarr
" sitting hand in hand before the fire " and ended
with Dowson and Plarr embracing.*

But Plarr was then dead, and could not remark
upon this article, nor upon his daughter's biographical
novel 'Cynara', which contained eight of Dowson's
letters to him (either in full or in part), letters which
he had withheld in 1914, and of which he had written :
" Alas ! the reticence, which is perhaps the quintes-
sence of criticism and biography, compels me to omit
passages, nay to suppress whole letters of great beauty,
which some ruthless hand may give to the Press a
century hence."

Plarr had considered, with nice feeling, that it
would desecrate the Dowson sanctuary to print letters
in which the poet confessed that Adelaide made the
blood dance in his veins whenever she spoke or smiled
or moved, or admitted that he was " far too absorbed
to do anything but sit, in Poland, and gather the
exquisite moments ". But when a legend has grown
" half diabolic " through falsification of fact, and the
atmosphere is sinister with whispers, Plarr might have
been bold enough to allow Dowson to speak for
himself. For that matter, Miss Plarr might have been
so bold also, and not buried in the darnel waste of her
imaginative fiction such new extracts as she selected.

* Mr. Herbert Palmer has now given this anecdote additional
prominence by reprinting it in his 'Post-Victorian Poetry', 1938.

As it is, we still await the publication of the complete
Dowson-Plarr correspondence, annotated without
bias, and with the assurance of unabridgment.

Miss Plarr's book being published as fiction, it is
sufficient to regret its publication. Her novel will
naturally affect the legend (just as Miss May Sinclair's
' Divine Fire ' or Mrs. Atherton's ' The Gorgeous
Isle ', novels, said to be suggested by Dowson's
career, must have affected it), but, it is to be hoped,
less drastically than if, in its present form, it had
appeared as a biography.

In the same year that saw the publication of Miss
Plarr's work of fiction, 1933, Mr. Edgar Jepson,
Dowson's remaining champion, published his
' Memories of a Victorian '. The trend that opinion
was taking had not passed by him unnoticed. In his
answers to Mr. Symons, already quoted, he answered
those commentators who had been so influenced by
Mr. Symons. But there was still a reply needed to
Sir William Rothenstein's suggestion that " Dowson
meant deliberately to hurt himself. . . . I doubt
if Dowson wanted to live ". Mr. Jepson had no such
doubts, and said so with the bluntness of authority :
" In his Memoirs Professor Rothenstein speaks of
Dowson's deliberately destroying himself. He is
wrong."

Mr. Desmond Flower, in the introduction to his
valuable enlarged edition of ' The Poetical Works ',
1934, appeared also to believe that the ill-reports
were exaggerations or inventions. He, too, criticized
Mr. Symons' biographical details and synthetic
Bohemianism, and expressed the certain opinion that
Dowson's heart was not in Limehouse.

And here, in the fact of being repulsed by two staunch defenders, I wish I could leave the myth ; but, unfortunately, neither of these gentlemen has had the last word.

In 1936 two books appeared. In one, ' John Lane and the Nineties ', by Mr. J. Lewis May, we find these remarks : " Dowson, with his fondness for coffee-stalls and cabmen's shelters and for the girl in the ' Sceptre ', was in a strong position. . . ." and : " Francis Thompson did not, in his day, share the popularity enjoyed by Phillips and Dowson. Five hundred copies—not ten thousand—were printed of the first edition. . . ."

Dowson in a *strong* position in the 90's ! Dowson in his day selling ten thousand copies ! We can pass over the girl in the " Sceptre " (the barmaid in " The Crown " is a possible solution, Adelaide in " Poland " the probable one) as an inaccurate remembrance of gossip ; but that while Dowson lived he was a " best-seller " must, in all fairness, be denied. Let us allow bibliographical facts to answer Mr. May's fantasy.

The truth of the matter is this. " In his day " Dowson published three books of poetry : ' Verses,' 1896, limited to 330 copies ; ' The Pierrot of the Minute ', 1897, limited to 330 copies ; and ' Decorations ', 1899, issued by the same publisher, of which it is believed no more than 330 copies were issued. The editions of these three books, then, added together fall short of one thousand copies. And not one of them was reprinted during Dowson's lifetime. Indeed, they were not over-subscribed at the time of his death, 1900, for we find their publisher, Leonard Smithers, giving them away generously to all and sundry in that year as mementoes.

Again, with regard to this question of popular demand and concomitant value, inscribed presentation copies from Dowson were offered at some three shillings apiece in booksellers' catalogues in the opening years of this century.

The second book, published in 1936, 'Aspects of Wilde ', by Mr. Vincent O'Sullivan, bears out these assertions, and confutes further the suggestions made by Mr. Lewis May of Dowson's " strong position " and " ten thousand copies " in his day.

"All the verse or prose," Mr. O'Sullivan remarks on one page, " that Dowson cared to produce, Smithers was ready to publish, Smithers and no one else in London." And on another : " During Dowson's lifetime nobody but Smithers would look at him."

These facts are important, and, one does not doubt, reliable, for Smithers was Mr. O'Sullivan's publisher at that time as well as Dowson's. It is a pity, therefore, that they were not all that Mr. O'Sullivan desired to record. Instead, he went on to provide eight closely printed pages of gossip and reminiscence detrimental to Dowson's character. These pages, fortunately, or unfortunately, at once call to mind those of Mr. Symons, of Frank Harris, and of Mr. Yeats. In them, the impossibility of Dowson's resisting endless drinking is again touched upon, and the now familiar phrases " mean drink-shops ", " poisonous liquor ", " gutter appearance " reappear. Like Mr. Yeats, Mr. O'Sullivan speaks of an *Italian* restaurant, but, more definite than Mr. Yeats, is certain that " St. Francis de

Sales and John Wesley rolled together . . . would not have succeeded in prevailing upon Dowson to see any charm in a sober, godly and tranquil life."

And there you have the case-history of the Dowson myth, defamation heavily out-weighing support at every turn ; his acquaintances all of the firm opinion that the poet was a confirmed drug-taker, debauchee, wastrel and raving dipsomaniac ; yet those who knew him well refusing to admit this summation.

Let me now read you the newly-discovered and unpublished material, to which I referred earlier, Dowson's letters to an Oxford friend, the dedicatee of the poet's ' Beata Solitudo ', and the translator for Beardsley's ' Lysistrata '.

It is my belief that a small measure of psychological insight expended by you on the vocabulary, phraseology, and, above all, the general tone of these twelve letters will reveal the true character of their writer.

Having examined a considerable amount of evidence, and considered its fluctuations and metamorphoses, in a search for the truth, I am now prepared to side with Plarr and Mr. Jepson in their reasonable good opinion ; with the reservation, however, that Dowson's careless mode of living and indifference to the expectations of society laid him open, perhaps, to a tithe of the criticism and reproach that he has received.

If I can influence a reconsideration of the ill-opinion of his character that some of you must hold, this inspection of his personal affairs will, I dare hope, be justified.

IV.

The first letter, written from Church End, Woodford, in the early spring of 1891, contains a reference to the ' Cynara ' poem, but, significantly, no mention of the twelve-year-old Adelaide :

> " I have seen the proofs of my ' Cynara ' poem, for the April *Hobby*. It looks less indecent in print, but I am still nervous ! though I admire Horne's audacity. I read it, or rather Lionel [Johnson] did for me, at the last Rhymers. . . . I have just read through the VIth 'Æneid ' ; and am intoxicate with its adorable phrases. After all, with all our labour of the file and chisel we cannot approach these people, in this gross tongue.

> "*Sunt lacrimae rerum et mentem mortalia tangunt.*
> *Umbrarum hic locus est, Somni Noctisque soporae.*
> *Discedam, explebo numerum, reddarque tenebris.*
> *I decus, i, nostrum : melioribus utere fatis.*

> "On to the last couplet, by the way, I have tagged a sonnet entitled ' To a Child, growing out of Childhood and Away ! '—a real *Hobby Horse* title I swear, which I will show you hereafter."

The absence of all mention of Adelaide in this letter is not the only significant point. Dowson admits that a Vergilian couplet has inspired him to a sonnet. He speaks of the Latin poets collectively as " these people ", pointing to the probability that he has recently been engaged in reading them. Is not the Horatian phrase from the first Ode of the fourth book, then, the sole genesis of ' Cynara ', as it is its title ? The phrase excited Dowson's imagination to such a degree that he honoured it with a new poem. Indeed, in the act of composition, he no doubt bore Herbert Horne's *Hobby Horse* in mind as its publisher, as he does here, when entitling his new sonnet. I cannot believe differently.

The second letter, addressed from his father's office on Bridge Dock, Limehouse, fourteen months later, May 13th, 1892, I will not trouble to quote in full. It is merely an invitation, and its only interest lies in the fact that it shows that Dowson, in the interval, has become sufficiently intimate with Adelaide to call her " Missie " :

> " CARO MIO,
> ". . . Unfortunately I have arranged to dine at home on Wednesday night next, having asked some men round. Can't you manage to join me there at 8 or thereabouts ? You shall have some whist. Otherwise tomorrow and Thursday I shall be dining in Poland and enchanted to see you : but try to come on Wednesday, or if you are early enough over with the Academy come and call for me in Poland at 6 o'c. and we might manage 50 up before I wend my way home. Missie has gone back lately to Mme. L. and is generally kept there till 8 : so I do not amuse myself too much there nowadays . . ."

The third letter, written some months later in the early autumn of the same year, 1892, speaks for itself, revealing Dowson no longer in any mood of amusement :

> " I go on in precisely the same situation in Poland. I can't somehow screw myself up to making a declaration of myself to *Madame,* although I am convinced it is the most reasonable course. Any day however with favourable

omens it may arrive. She herself is sometimes very charming, sometimes not! But in the latter case it is merely my own abominably irritable temper which is to blame. I have had an interview of abnormal length with Lionel [Johnson], in which he argued with me most strenuously all night. He had been dining at my Uncle's (the Hooles), and apparently this infatuation of mine was openly discussed the whole of dinner-time *par tous ces gens.* So I do not see how it can go on very much longer without an understanding or a *fracas*—the latter I suppose will be inevitable first—with my people. Altogether *Je m'embête horriblement ;* and my only consolation is that if it is so obvious to all my friends and relatives it ought to be equally so to the Poles as well. ' Masquerade ' [' A Comedy of Masks '] is now under consideration with Bentley : the first publishers it has yet been to. If the result is favourable I really think I shall be inspired to make the disagreeable necessary overtures in Poland. Another year of the stress and tension and uncertainty of these last 6 months will leave me without a nerve in my composition and I am not sure whether I have any now."

In the fourth letter, written probably two months later in December, 1892, Dowson announces progress in his love affair:

"I have been existing in a curiously tense state for the last month or so, and for the last week tense is scarcely the word. It is better than the old stagnation, but it is exhausting. Things are coming to a crisis, *cher vieux!* I go to have *tête-à-tête* teas with *Madame* ! We talk intimately, we talk of Her—*natürlich*—and we are constantly on the verge of an understanding. Yesterday it was the nearest shave of all. She gave me an admirable occasion. I am sure she expected it. I was just coming out with a protestation, to the effect that my one object and desire in life was to be of service to her admirable daughter—when we were interrupted. We were both curiously moved ! I went out and had a gin and bitters and poured it tremulously down my shirt, and passed a perfectly wide-awake night—damning the interruption. This morning I saw that it would have been foolish ; but this afternoon I shall be in precisely the same state, and I feel certain that it is only a question of days now. To think that a little girl of barely fourteen should have so disorganized my spiritual economy.

" I should like to see you and hear your advice, though of course unless it agreed with my own, however good it were, I shouldn't take it. It is a difficult case. If it were not for the complication of a foreign point of view and foreign traditions—I should be justified in waiting, in holding my tongue. Only when one remembers how very much earlier abroad these matters are arranged— and especially in Germany—the case is changed. An English mother would be scandalised at your proposing for the hand of her daughter before she were 16 ; a foreign mother might reasonably be equally scandalised if you were attentive to her daughter, without making your mind clear to her, at a much earlier age. But there are objections either way. . . . I should like to see you, for verily, this matter grievously weighs me down."

A new phase in Dowson's emotional predicament began with the illness and subsequent death of "Missie's" father, Joseph Foltinowicz, in the spring of 1893.

The fifth letter, written from the office on Bridge Dock at this time, describes the poet's "declaration" and manner in which it was received :

"CHER AMI,

" Let me preface this by saying that it is strictly private and confidential ; and so proceed to inform you of certain recent developments in my affairs. I fancy, when I last saw you, you must have been about the beginning of the rather distressful state of things which augmented itself later on. I daresay I was not very brilliant society then—(I don't remember frankly, much about our *rencontre*)—and certainly I have been too much absorbed to write letters ever since or I would have written to you. I suppose it will not surprise you very much to hear that I have at last unburdened myself. We were all in rather a stressful state of nerves—and Missie herself rather brought it about by her curious changes of mood—sometimes she was perfectly charming, at others she would hardly speak to me. *Quid plura dicam ?* Finally I was goaded into a declaration—of course it was rather an inopportune time, the father having been given up by the doctors—but on the other hand, I don't suppose except for the rather tense state we were in on this account, I should have been so precipitate. She took it with a great deal of dignity and self-possession ; I don't think I have ever admired her more. She reminded me very properly that she was rather too young : but she proceeded to admit that she was not surprised at what I had told her, and that she was not angry. Of course I had asked her for no answer—I merely left her with no possible reason to doubt my seriousness in the matter. Finally I suggested that she should forget what I had said for the present—and that we should resume our ancient relation and be excellent friends—and nothing more. Upon this understanding we separated. The next day—after twelve of about as miserable hours as I hope to spend—it seemed to me that I had upset the whole arrangement—a conversation with *Madame* reassured me. Nothing could possibly exceed her extreme kindness and delicacy. She didn't in the least appear to resent, as she might very reasonably have resented, my proposing to her daughter, without her permission a couple of days before her 15th birthday ; on the contrary she seemed rather pleased—in short, she was perfect. Moreover she gave me every hope—she said that Missie had told her she would like the idea in a year or two:—only just then she was naturally strung up and disordered by her father's state. According to *Madame* it will arrange itself. You may imagine how this pleased and touched me. All this was on or about the 15th ; on Monday last Foltinowicz died—yesterday I attended his funeral. I have seen Missie on or off pretty much as usual during this time—and I have not alluded to the important subject. We are both a little embarrassed—I more than she perhaps—and sometimes she drives me to despair by her coldness. At other times she is charming : *Madame* is always mercifully the same—I think on the whole, the most gentle and delicate minded lady whom I may hope to meet in this disagreeable world. And so, *mon cher ami*, it stands, my affair. *Qu'en pensez-vous ?* I entreat you to write to me. I don't know how it will end—I hope at least that the embarrassment, the *gêne* which I have produced, entirely through my own hastiness, will wear off. It has been an exhausting three weeks—I feel as if I had been travelling all the time, sleeping in my clothes, lacking beds and baths. On the whole it is a relief to me to have the air clear—at any rate *Madame* thoroughly understands the situation. For the rest I am not very sanguine ; if she liked me less or had not known me so long, I believe, my chance would be much better. She has a very difficult character, but at the same time a very fine one ; exceedingly fond of her as I have been, I was amazed to see her during the last difficult week—that immensely trying time which has to elapse between a death and a burial—quite the cruellest part of death—she was intensely distressed and worn out, and perfectly composed. It was the same at the cemetery, when extraneous womankind were dissolved in tears, she stood like a little statue. At the same time I know that when she has been alone, she has had paroxysms of weeping, and this is a child of fifteen. I am afraid I am making large draughts upon your patience. But I may as well exhaust myself completely.

" It is a very odd history—Heaven knows how it will end. In my more rational moments however, I am inclined to consider that that is of quite secondary importance ; the important thing is that one should have, just once, experienced this mystery, an absolute absorption in one particular person. It reconciles all inconsistencies in the order of things, and above all it seems once and for all to reduce to utter absurdity any material explanation of itself or of the world. I will try and finish some verses I am working on and enclose upon this matter, to-night. I wish you were down here ; we must meet soon—but we might have an excellent symposium here, in this extraordinary place of silence, with only river sounds. When you come to Poland, not a word of this, but I hope you will not have anything unusual to notice, except the absence of *ce pauvre monsieur's* cap and coat. What an infinitely dreary thing by the way is a London funeral. We make death more hideous than it need be. As they treated the old Vikings we should be sent out into a stormy sea in a burning ship. That distressing delay, and wearisome *cortège*, and the pit-a-pat of earth on the coffin are cruelties which civilization should spare one. I suppose however that no amount of euphemism will affect the essential horror of the thing or make it a less inexplicable cruelty. I have been interested to note—I have had various occasions lately—the immediate revulsion of life against death, which occurs after the disposal of the body, amongst persons who have been weighed down by the sincerest grief : this is quite universal and well worth consideration. A sort of instinctive protest against the thought of death by healthy life : consciously justifying itself ? Or may it not be really the result of a more generous instinct—that actually death is not an essential fact, but an accident of immortality—so that what seems such cruel dishonour to a beloved person, all the corruption of death, is outside his interest or ours, I don't mean that this is rigidly apprehended—but is it not an innate feeling ? You really must forgive me this prosing, I shall frighten you from my society. This letter is like *Tristan and Isolde*, it has nothing but love and death in it. I assure you there are still other things upon which I can discourse.

> " *Au revoir,*
>> "Ever yours,
>>> "ERNEST DOWSON."

The sixth letter, a year later, shows little change in the position :

> " Bridge Dock,
>> " Maundy Thursday,
>>> 1894.

" You are right, I fear, when you draw my horoscope. But the Ides are not yet. *Quod bene eveniat !* One lives and talks as if the making of many books were the end and aim of all things. I am afraid they are the straws one chews to cheat one's appetite. Whether the Ides come a little sooner or a little later, they must come this year. I always have a sort of feeling upon me that I am doing certain things for the last time. Therefore I am particularly anxious for you to come to Brittany with me this year. . . . I must have one month more in Brittany before the Ides if only you could manage it. Noah must have had somewhat similar emotions to mine when he began to build his Ark. Out of what am I to build one ? I am afraid I must trust to my swimming powers. In Poland there is no material alteration— perhaps we are a little troubled by the approach of anniversaries."

It is a strange and prophetic coincidence that Dowson speaks here of feeling that he was doing certain things for the last time, for it must have been about this date, the spring of 1894, that phthisis, a disease which usually runs a course of six years, gripped him.

And the mention of the Ides was prophetic also ;

for in the twenty-one months that elapsed between
this and the seventh letter, they duly arrived, accompanied by every form of disaster. The dry-dock at
Limehouse failed. The poet's parents committed
suicide in quick succession, his father taking an
overdose of chloral, his mother hanging herself. And
without home or worldly prospects, Dowson began to
wander the face of the earth.*

V.

Undermined in health, he yet continued his literary
output. And, while there seemed no hope in the
immediate future of a union with Missie, his love for
her persisted as strongly as ever.

Late in 1895 Dowson is in Paris, at 214, rue St.
Jacques. He has fled abroad after a crisis. The
seventh letter is in reply to his friend's inquiries :

> " You mustn't imagine, as I gather from your letter
> you perhaps did, that my ' crisis ' was sentimental. God
> forbid. I have just answered my *damigella's* last letter
> and we are on the most affectionate terms—at least I
> think so—that we have been on for years. You must
> go and see her when you are in London—*please* do that,
> and speak of me as freely as you like, *only do not* speak of
> my exile as being so prolonged as I presume it will be.
> I always write to her with the intention of returning in a
> month or two—and so I may—*for a fortnight !* but I
> doubt if ever I shall make my home in England again.
> My great desire is that the Foltinowiczs will carry out
> their long-conceived idea of returning to Germany. Then

---

* Here, I might point out, was every excuse for Dowson to drink
heavily, if he so desired. Here were the excuses that Mr. Symons might
have proffered and Mr. Talcott Williams, who desired mitigating
circumstances, would have accepted But until 1933 these facts were
withheld, Plarr, in 1914, stating—" of the sudden deaths of the poet's
father and mother I am expressly forbidden to write ".

I would go there and join them. But I have taken a great dislike to London. I really came away on a sort of mad impulse—which I have not since regretted— because I was financially broke and . . . somewhat sensationally I admit, but not in the state of desperation which I believe is rumoured about me. *Par exemple*, dear Marmie [Marmaduke Langdale, actor], who has written me letters full of the most noble offers and sentiments writes to me in his last, received two days ago : ' I have created a sort of mist of trouble, vague as ghosts in a dream, with which I surround you. It forms a sort of halo of sorrow for you and excites the tears and sympathy of those who live and admire you from afar ! ! ! '

" *Do* tell him (don't show him this letter) *do* suggest to him, without hurting his feelings, for I know he has really a great affection for me, and it pleases him to give me an ' atmosphere ', that I don't want no halo of this kind and extremely object to being wept over, I am not remarkably prosperous nor particularly happy—who is ? But I *do not* go about in Paris with a halo of ghosts and tears, having been gifted by God with a sense—common to you and myself but to how many other of our friends ? —of humour ! I occasionally smile, and even in Paris, at a late hour of the night, and Paris is later than London, have been known to laugh.

" Write soon, *mon très cher*, I implore you. And if you see Missie, tell her to write to me often, and if you could convey to her, not *from* me, but as an expression of your own personal opinion that to get a letter from her is my chiefest pleasure in life, you will be doing me a favour, and falling short of the extreme truth which perhaps it is not yet seasonable to say."

Paris suited Dowson, but not his pocket. In an unpublished letter to Mr. Jepson, written at this time, he confesses : " My news is of the scantiest ; beyond the obvious fact that I am, and have been, for some

5 weeks in Paris, and that *j'y probablement resterai.*
That is to say, unless you feel inclined to try Brittany
with me in another month. The Hotel Gloanec,
Pontaven, Finistère . . . offers board and lodging, including cider for 85 francs a month. I should
be strongly tempted to try this for two or three
months in company ; therefore think it over. . . ."
And, later in this same letter from Paris, he continues :
" I find I can do considerably more work here than in
town, and if I can keep it up, and do not find it too
expensive would prefer to remain here than hibernate
in the country. . . . I am really working very
hard and find every moment occupied."

I have interpolated these extracts with some design ;
for we have come to the period of the suggested
dreadful debaucheries about *Les Halles,* and approach
that of Mrs. Atherton's memories, Dowson's stay at
Pont Aven, whence he moved alone (for Mr. Jepson
was unable to join him) in the early spring of 1896 ;
moved, I think it is clear, to continue uninterrupted
his writing for *The Savoy,* his translation of ' La
Pucelle ' for Leonard Smithers, and the preparation
for press of his first book of poetry, ' Verses '. Indeed,
to Plarr he wrote on arriving in Brittany : " I feel
I shall do much work here. . . . I felt rested
and restored to some prospect of reasonable health
directly I came here."

But to return to the series of Dowson's letters to his
Oxford friend.

The eighth, ninth, tenth and eleventh are all
addressed from the Hotel Gloanec ; the eleventh in
all likelihood at about the time Mrs. Atherton
encountered Mr. Vachell there.

Here is the eighth letter, probably written in February, 1896 :

> " I sent off a story, written here, the other day to it, [*The Savoy*], but it may not be in time for the forthcoming number. In any case it will include the following ['In a Breton Cemetary'] or another poem—for I have sent them a choice of two.
>
> " Yes : I deeply regret that I shall not be in Paris to receive you ; but let us hope it is only the postponement of a *réunion* which we will have here. How did you like doing the ' Lysistrata ' ? Smithers offered it to me, but I funked it. I hope you get on with him. He is, all round, the best fellow I know, and it is astonishing to me how many people fail to see this, or seeing it temporarily (instance Conder, Rothenstein *inter alios*) succeed in quarrelling with him."

The ninth letter, despatched the next month, March, 1896, refers to the dedication to Adelaide of ' Verses ' :

> " I hope the dedication of my poems will be understood of her and accepted—as, although there is no name, nor initials even, it will doubtless be understood of others— who will not, I hope, think it extravagant. It is very literally true."

In the tenth note, written shortly after Easter, 1896, Dowson refers again to his dedication to which, in all likelihood in proof, he had added Missie's christian name—" Adelaide " :

> " I have asked Smithers to give you a copy of ' Verses ' which may be out by the time this reaches you. Let me know how you find them, and if you think the ' Preface ' is indiscreet."

In the eleventh letter, dated " *In : fest. Corp : Christi*", 1896. Dowson is more communicative :

> " I am glad you like the volume. Do you like Aubrey Beardsley's binding-block ? I am very pleased with it. There are no reviews yet, but I have had very charming letters from [John] Gray, Teixera [de Mattos] and [Arthur] Symons, the last of whom, as also Yeats, are going to write about it. Perhaps, you are right in your remarks about my preface. Conal [O'Riordan] is dedicating to me his new novel 'A Fool and His Heart ' and I fear the dedication is appropriate. But it is too late to convert me now ; I am idolatrous for the rest of my days. Idolatrous to the extent that Keats was when he wrote from Rome to his friend Browne : ' the lining which she put in my travelling cap *scalds* my head '—and like Keats I can not open her letters for a day or so after they reach me. There is nothing in the universe which you can do, which will give me more pleasure than to pay the visit of which you speak. I have not yet sent her the volume, as the large-paper copies will not be bound for another week. . . .
>
> " Well, enough : it grows near post-time. Go and see my Missie I beseech you : and tell me how she takes my ' Preface '—if she reads it. I only ask that she does not *m'en vouloir* for it, and that is a little thing to ask for as absolute an adoration as any girl or woman has ever had from anyone."

The twelfth, and last letter, was sent nearly a year later, in the spring of 1897 from the Foltinowicz restaurant, " Poland ", when Dowson had returned to England on a visit. At this time the issue had passed from the poet to the waiter, whom Missie married that September. And the real agony of Dowson's mind is only too apparent :

" I know you must think me a fool, but I am suffering the torture of the damned. I ought to have drowned myself at Pont Aven, or having come back to London I ought to have had the strength of mind to have kept away. Now, if I change my rooms or go to the Arctic Pole it is only an increased intolerable Hell, and except yourself, and slightly, Morse, there is not a person I come across who realizes that I am being scorched daily, or does not put down my behaviour to sheer ill humour. *Quousque tandem, Domine, quousque tandem ?* "

Three years later Dowson's phthisis conquered him.

VI.

I have read you intimate letters, letters more personal than those Victor Plarr published in 1914, but the words he prefaced to his correspondence, I think, might fit these equally well : " In these letters," wrote Plarr, " no ugly slur of passion, no ill savours are to be found. Instead, we are refreshed by fragrance—transient and slight, perhaps, yet evident—by fragrance, be it said again, and by an unfailing touch of good breeding, a gracious and insistent air of modesty—by something diffident, boyishly shy, often beautiful and noble."

ALEXANDER PETŐFI.

By Sandor von Hegedüs.

[Read April 27th, 1938.]

It was about midnight on December 31st, 1822, when all hearts were beating to greet 1823, that in the town of Kiskörös Alexander Petőfi first opened his eyes. Possibly it matters little whether he was born in one year or another ; we are satisfied to know that he lived and belonged to us. No one stops to inquire when the stars were born. What we delight in is that they are there in the sky and as bright as always. A comet is Petőfi ! He rose from an unknown section of the people; he vanished in an unmarked grave. He was the child of the people. One might compare him with Burns. But Petőfi's parents were constantly travelling and not bound to one particular place, whereas Burns's people lived in one spot. What concerns us most is the child's environment. Like Burns, Petőfi saw daylight under a thatched roof. And this was their luck. They came closer to nature and to their own people so.

Petőfi's childish impressions run through his poems. His playmates and associations are the shepherd, the swallows that fly around his parents' hut, the stork that makes its nest on the roof, the great swamps, the infinite pusztas, the idle ferry, the abandoned draw-well ; then all children's delight—the mirage, the rainbow's lovely glitter, the winds that seem to drive away the dragons, the hail-storms and the somewhat milder winter wind that comes as a blessing after

heavy snow. Petőfi learnt from Nature. He says:
" There is no secret of Nature I do not know. We
understand each other. That is why we are such
good friends. I understand and enjoy the song of
the brook, the roaring of the river, the hissing of the
wind and the journeying of the clouds. . . . I
have been taught poetry by the grammar of world
mysteries. In particular I understand the rustle of
the leaves. I sit down beneath a tree and listen for
hours to the sounds they give, to the fairy tales they
whisper into my ears. They swing the soul into a
balmy dream, and seem to give expression to the
imagination as if through the chime of magic bells—
calling thus to the angels of heaven to enter my
heart, this little chapel of mine."

No one could have defined Petőfi's relationship to
Nature better. Never was there a poet in Hungary
who could so well project his mother country upon
the eyes of the world as Petőfi interpreted Hungary.
It was through Petőfi that the world came to know of
her pusztas, sand-hills, winding rivers, woodlands
and hills, her flower-gardens. But his wandering
life was necessary to make a complete synthesis of
the country viewed from Nature's standpoint.

As a child he was restless. He could not stay in
one school. He first entered the Piarist School in
Pest. From the wooden benches in the classroom
his eyes gazed over the Danube embankment, and
possibly the spot where later his bronze statue was
to stand. After the Piarists he was sent to Aszód,
then to Selmecz. Both are small towns in Upper
Hungary. But he could not endure school discipline.
Leaving his school in Selmecz, he came back to

Pest on foot. No soft walking in those days ! Fate
never destined Petőfi for pillows ; his portion was to
be suffering and struggle. These two things developed
his soul and his creative thinking. His first job in
Pest was on the stage of the National Theatre as a
super ; he also sold programmes. Think of Shakespeare's early days ! His fondness for Shakespeare is
best expressed by him, when he says : "After God
Shakespeare created most in life." Petőfi's restless
soul drove him away again. He went to the city
of Sopron and enlisted as a soldier. But he was
not made for military discipline. They made him
carry wood and take water into the kitchen. When he
was on duty he used to scribble poems on the sentry-
box. Edgar Allan Poe wrote his poems on a wooden
door of an inn. He was a soldier for only one and
a half years. His regiment moved on to Graz,
where he caught typhoid fever in March, 1840.

During his sickness a kind-hearted army doctor
discovered his abilities as a poet, and pleaded for
his release. He got it. He was free again. It was
in March, 1841, with his discharge in his pocket, he
started for home from Károlyváros, a town in Croatia.
He still had fever, a weak constitution, and had lost
weight. His blue trousers were tucked into his high
boots ; he had a blue military coat and a white fur
cap. When he arrived at the Hungarian border his
eyes wandered over the country he so much loved.
And whilst he was thinking, Fate whispered, " I will
give you eight heavy and rich years—my child, my
youth—eight years in which you will reach the highest
pinnacle of genius. During this short period you
will give expression to everything that for thousands

of years has been hidden deep in the soul of your own people. As a reward for your wanderings, sufferings and restlessness I will give you two things, a flaming life and an early death!" Life gave him thus eight more years. Petőfi after his return did not know what to begin. He was just seventeen years old. He went to school again to Pápa in the Transdanubian region. He met Mauris Jókai here, the greatest Hungarian story-teller, with whom he formed a close friendship. They both dreamt of immortality. They read together the works of Shakespeare, Dickens, Dumas, Walter Scott and Victor Hugo. These poets influenced their writings. Petőfi was still undecided whether acting would suit him best. At one time he thought that immortality means applause.

Later he said he was a forsaken little travelling actor, for whom neither God nor man cared at all. Besides poverty, sickness! It was during this that he collected his poems, and decided to go to Budapest on foot—his most miserable journey. To quote him : " I started out in worn-out clothes and with a volume of poems under my arm. I had a few pennies on me. All my hope lay in my poems. I said to myself: 'If I sell them, all well and good. If I do not sell them, it is the same. Then at least I will freeze and die hungry. My sufferings will then come to an end.' I was alone. I did not meet a soul. Everyone was under cover " (it was February) " because of the weather. The wind blew all the rain into my face. My tears became frozen. . . . After one week's journey I arrived in Budapest. I had more or less come to the end of my reserves. Desperate courage took charge of me. I went to one of the

most famous men in Hungary. I felt I was playing
my last trump card—Life or Death." Petőfi went
to see Michael Vörösmarty, then the greatest poet
and one of the finest men in Hungary. This great
man immediately recognized his ability, entertained
him like a brother, gave him money and edited his
poems. With this act Petőfi's wanderings came to
an end. The lure of the stage was no more, and,
though often called back, he never trod it again.

From now on he wants to be a poet only. This is in
1844. And his rise to fame is very quick. He
achieves what he longed for in his school, on the stage
and in soldier's boots—fame. His writings are known
all through the country. He idolizes love and
liberty ; to quote his motto :

> " Liberty, Love !
> These two I need.
> For love I sacrifice
> My life,
> For liberty I sacrifice
> My love."

And these are not just mere words. In them we
find his soul, his real personality. The single explanation for his fame is the fact that people feel that he is
only telling the truth and nothing but the truth.
He believed in love, liberty, and the immortality of
the Hungarian race. The power of not giving in,
which he had abundantly inherited, was the strength
of the Hungarian race.

Petőfi's rise to fame then starts with the year 1844,
when literary circles admit him. He moves in society,
and here he meets his first love—Etelka Csapó. He
spends Christmas in her house and is happy. Fate

however interferes again. The beloved dies in a few days, quite unexpectedly. He is stricken; never has death crept so close to him.

His job is now Assistant Editor of the 'Pest Fashion Journal'. Through this association he meets new people. He starts writing poems with a political tendency. There was no freedom of the Press at this time in Hungary. The restrictions of the Austrian censor drove him more and more into singing the glory of freedom, the glory of his country and the glory of the war of independence. In speaking of liberty, he thought of world-liberty for all peoples. It is interesting to note that Louis Kossuth, the great Hungarian statesman and hero of liberty, who started the revolution of 1848 against the Habsburgs, preached the same subject. A small nation like the Magyars gave two great geniuses to the world at the same time, men who, a hundred years in advance of their own age, while fighting for the liberty of their own people yet represent a higher ideal.

Petőfi's collected poems were first published in 1846. In the preface he gives a true account of himself : " God has not provided for me, that I may spend my life with time in pleasant parks listening to the nightingales, and sing amidst the hush of leaves and the rustle of brooks, or that I may meditate on silent happiness or silent pain. My life has been performed on the battle-field, on the field of sufferings and passions, where the corpses of good old days lie, where murdered hopes are murdering death ; ironic laughs of unattained wishes, amidst bewitched hisses of disillusions, my Muse sings a song in a half conscious

state, as a condemned princess on an island, in the
Land Beyond, which is guarded by wild animals and
monsters." This period was one of great depression
for Petőfi. "Fate, open the way for me, let me do
something for mankind!" he cries.

He leaves for the country again in the year 1846.
He is tired and wants inspiration from Nature. This
is given to him by his motherland—Nature refreshes
him, and he starts out again for new laurels. He was
staying in a country town in Nagykároly, and it so
happened that the inn in which he was staying was
opposite the house of the agent of the Count Károlyi's
estates. Here he saw Julia Szendrey for the first
time. They were married a year after their meeting,
on September 8th, 1847.

They spent their honeymoon in the castle of the
counts Teleky in Koltó. In a very restless life these
few weeks count as the most undisturbed period.
Living for the happiness of his bride here in the park
in Koltó, he felt like a king in retirement, because he
had entered the golden empire of happiness—a feeling
hitherto unexperienced. In one of his letters he
writes of this change as follows: "From this time
on I count my life the existence of the world. Before
this time I was nowhere; there was no world, there
was nothing. Only then did the million worlds
become created and love installed in my heart!"

In this state he writes his lovely poem, 'At the
end of September', not only a pearl among Hungarian
lyrics, but among the world's. Here he is already a
prophet, because he foresees his early death, and
desires his wife, if she forgets him on account
of another man's love, to put the widow's veil on his

cross, for then he will come up from the graveyard world and will wipe away his tears with this veil : " One who even there and even then loves you for ever."

His honeymoon is soon over. He has to return to the city, to his desk in the editorial office. A dull task after such a happy time ! Now all Europe was in a ferment. Everyone felt that there must be a change, big times in the making, because the century was struck with new ideas. Petőfi announced with inspired belief that revolution would break out. He did write a few poems addressed to his wife and commenting on happy marriage, but most of his time was taken up by political and revolutionary poems.

The February French Revolution in the year 1848 was decisive. It fired Louis Kossuth, the great Hungarian hero of independence, to call to arms the Hungarian nation against suppression by the Habsburgs. The revolution broke out on March 15th in Budapest. It meant the secession from the Habsburgs, Hungary's independence, freedom of the serfs, freedom of the Press and the legitimate use of the Hungarian language. Hectic days ! We see Petőfi side by side with the nation's leader Kossuth, announcing with all his fervent spirit that the day of freedom has arrived. His most impressive patriotic poem, 'To arms, Magyar!'—(Stand up, Magyar!)—he recites on this day from the steps of the National Museum ; then he goes with Jókai, the immortal Hungarian story-teller, to the printing house, and they themselves set the type, drive the Habsburg censors away, and, as the first production of the free press, distribute copies of this poem among the people. Thus the two boyhood friends—Petőfi and Jókai—

become the heroes of Hungarian independence. They join Kossuth and give impetus to the 1848 Hungarian war of independence. Kossuth's genius awakens the nations, the national militiamen rally under the flag, Görgey trains them to become an army, and conquers the Austrian forces of occupation in many a battle. The world at large follows excitedly the heroic deeds of the struggle, and Petőfi's songs are heard far and wide breaking through the noise of the battlefields.

The results of the war are familiar. The Habsburg dynasty, fearing the loss of its throne, seeks the aid of the Czar of all the Russias. He sends an army of 200,000 men, who enter the country to vanquish the Kossuth revolution. Petőfi bids farewell to his wife and his one-year-old son, and enters the army of General Bem, who is of Polish origin. They encounter the army of the Russian general Lueders near Segesvár in Transylvania. The fatal battle is on July 31st, 1849. This day he falls. On the morning of his death, at breakfast, he recites at the request of his inn-keeper his famous poem, ' Oh let me fall on the battlefield ! ' That same afternoon Lueders destroys the Hungarian army on the plains of Segesvár; everyone flees, because the Kozak troops have broken the Hungarian " Honvéds " (national militia). Petőfi is standing on a bridge, gazing into the deep waters, when his fleeing comrades warn him of the approach of the Kozaks ; but he only waves his hand, as if to denote the nothingness of living. His sole remark in answer to his friends is one word, "Rubbish ! ". A few minutes later the Kozaks chase him into a corn-field. He draws his sword and faces

the group. One of them transfixes him with his
lance. After the battle they bury the dead in a
common grave, among them him too, as if to follow
word for word his prophecy, " For you, sacred
Liberty, did we all die ". Then the Russian soldiers
step on his dead body.

This was Petőfi's life. There was never a poet who
could express his feelings so deeply, or who could paint
the sufferings and feelings of his race like him. Not
a set-back in his career ! Always a continuous rise in
fame ! And in the end he dies a martyr's death, a
privilege allotted alone to those whom God favours.
The question is often asked, " What would have
become of him if he had not died at the age of twenty-
six and a half ". The reply is very easy. He would
never have been greater, because he was the poet of
youth, and ended his life as a young man.

If we want to classify his poems, we can divide
them into lyrical, descriptive, political and narrative.
It is hard to say whether he was better in lyrical or
narrative poems. He substitutes for the then
fashionable classic metres and verse, forms which
were practically chained down by the weight of the
metres, the free, easy type of poetry, which he brings
up to perfection. He made the *song* classic. No
one could write poetry more easily than Petőfi, and
he was lucky in having had a restless life as part of
his fate, because through his wanderings he came to
know every section of his people. The old saying
came true again in the case of Petőfi, that only things
around us can become more inward and we can only
express these things. He did not sing anything more
than he himself saw. Stendhal demanded of the

realistic novel that it be a wandering looking-glass.
Petőfi achieves this in lyrics.   He describes everything
that appears before him—the Hungarian puszta (plain),
the shepherd, the brigand in exile, the meadows
encircled by the mirage, the winding river Theiss, the
surface of the water glittering in the sun, the orderly
rows of hay on the field, the skylark flying hither
and thither, the herd of cattle returning home, a
lonesome inn, and so forth.   His comparisons are
always drawn from Nature.   This love for Nature
derives from the French poet Lamartine.   He prized
his poems very much indeed.   No one has looked
deeper into nature than Petőfi has, when he says, " My
soul has been thrown into a giddy deep sweet maze,
even from the eternal beauty of nature ".   Or could
one speak more nobly of Nature than, " Oh nature,
how great art thou ! The more thou remain'st silent,
the more and the lovelier things thou say'st ".

His political poems reflect the struggles of his age,
the ideas of fermenting Europe.   He adored Béranger,
many of whose poems he translated.   He honoured
him as an apostle of Liberty and said of him, " The
sounds of cannons during the July Revolution are
the echoes of Béranger's name.   Everyone should
mention his sacred name with respect ! "   What
influenced him in Béranger was the love for liberty,
and not the poetry.   They dreamt, and Petőfi's
dream was the happy freedom of every man, the
dream of Shelley, in ' Prometheus Unbound '—a
general, a great freedom, world-liberty.   That Heine
and Byron come close to Petőfi's soul is to be
chiefly explained by their love of liberty, because
Petőfi was looking for that first of all.

Of his narrative poems, his ' Hero John ' is the most national. This is folk-lore poetry, a real epic, in which is fully expressed the spirit of the Hungarian race, its desires, sufferings, and even more, its dreams. ' Crazy Istok ' affects one as if he were describing his own life in it. The epic poem 'Apostle ' is written wholly under the influence of the French romanticists. The works of these writers impressed him when he was translating their works into Hungarian to earn a living.

When he was serving in the army at the age of seventeen he always carried Schiller's poems under his cap and a Horace in his cartridge-box. He adored his country, which he considered the world's loveliest land, or, to quote him : " If the world were God's hat, Hungary would be the crown of it."   He was always proud to have been of humble birth ; he loved the puszta-lowland.

As I have said, Burns stands closest to Petőfi ; but Petőfi's culture was of a higher calibre.   The fact that Petőfi was translating the great French and English classicists at the age of twenty shows this.

Petőfi will never pass away, because the strength of his soul is eternal.   We are a storm-ridden nation. We are broken up in every century, and then our great genius comes, a Rakoczi, a Kossuth, a Petőfi ; he puts spirit into us, and makes a nation of us again. That ancient strength, that lives in the Hungarian nation, in the Magyar race, that stubbornness revealed in this long-suffering people, these are within the soul of this poet:

" Immortal is the song and immortal is the Magyar ! "

CONTENTS OF VOLS. I—XVI.

VOL. I.

VOL. II.

VOL. III.

VOL. IV.

VOL. V.

VOL. VI.

VOL. VII.

VOL. VIII.

VOL. IX.

VOL. X.

VOL. XI.

VOL. XII.

VOL. XIII.

VOL. XIV.